THE HIGH DEEDS OF FINN

AND OTHER BARDIC ROMANCES OF ANCIENT IRELAND

BY

T. W. ROLLESTON

WITH AN INTRODUCTION
BY
STOPFORD A. BROOKE M.A. LL.D.

AR
CRAOIBH CONNARTHA NA GAEDHILGE
I NGLEANN FHAIDHLE BRONNAIM AN LEABHAR SEO:
BEANNACHT AGUS BUAIDH
LIBHSE GO DEO

ISBN-13:
978-1979880497

ISBN-10:
1979880492

THE HIGH DEEDS OF FINN

- Preface

Contents

Preface

The romantic tales here retold for the English reader belong neither to the category of folk-lore nor of myth, although most of them contain elements of both. They belong, like the tales of Cuchulain, which have been similarly presented by Miss Hull,[1] to the bardic literature of ancient Ireland, a literature written with an artistic purpose by men who possessed in the highest degree the native culture of their land and time. The aim with which these men wrote is also that which has been adopted by their present interpreter. I have not tried, in this volume, to offer to the scholar materials for the study of Celtic myth or folk-lore. My aim, however I may have fulfilled it, has been artistic, not scientific. I have tried, while carefully preserving the main outline of each story, to treat it exactly as the ancient bard treated his own material, or as Tennyson treated the stories of the MORT D'ARTHUR, that is to say, to present it as a fresh work of poetic imagination. In some cases, as in the story of the Children of Lir, or that of mac Datho's Boar, or the enchanting tale of King Iubdan and King Fergus, I have done little more than retell the bardic legend with merely a little compression; but in others a certain amount of reshaping has seemed desirable. The object in all cases has been the same, to bring out as clearly as possible for modern readers the beauty and interest which are either manifest or implicit in the Gaelic original.

For stories which are only found in MSS. written in the older forms of the language, I have been largely indebted to the translations published by various scholars. Chief among these (so far as the present work is concerned) must be named Mr Standish Hayes O'Grady—whose wonderful treasure-house of Gaelic legend, SILVA GADELICA, can never be mentioned by the student of these matters without an expression of admiration and of gratitude; Mr A.H. Leahy, author of HEROIC ROMANCES OF IRELAND; Dr Whitly Stokes, Professor Kuno Meyer, and M. d'Arbois de Jubainville, whose invaluable CYCLE MYTHOLOGIQUE IRLANDAIS has been much in my hands, both in the original and in the excellent English translation of Mr R.I. Best. Particulars of the source of each story will be found in the Notes on the Sources at the end of this volume. In the same place will also be found a pronouncing-index of proper names. I have endeavoured, in the text, to avoid or to modify any names which in their original form would baffle the English reader, but there remain some on the pronunciation of which he may be glad to have a little light.

The two most conspicuous figures in ancient Irish legend are Cuchulain, who lived—if he has any historical reality—in the reign of Conor mac Nessa immediately before the Christian era, and Finn son of Cumhal, who appears in literature as the captain of a kind of military order devoted to the service of the High King of Ireland during the third century A.D. Miss Hull's volume has been named after Cuchulain, and it is appropriate that mine should bear the name of Finn, as it is mainly devoted to his period; though, as will be seen, several stories belonging to other cycles of legend, which did not fall within the scope of Miss Hull's work, have been included here.[2] All the tales have been arranged roughly in chronological order. This does not mean according to the date of their composition, which in most cases is quite indiscoverable, and still less, according to the dates of the MSS. in which they are contained. The order is given by the position, in real or mythical history, of the events they deal with. Of course it is not practicable to dovetail them into one another with perfect accuracy. Where a story, like that of the Children of Lir, extends over nearly a thousand years, beginning with the mythical People of Dana and ending in the period of Christian monasticism, one can only decide on its place by considering where it will throw most light on those which come nearest to it. In this, as in the selection and treatment of the tales, there is of course room for much difference of opinion. I can only ask the critic to believe that nothing has been done in the framing of this collection of Gaelic romances without the consideration and care which the value of the material demands and which the writer's love of it has inspired.

T. W. ROLLESTON

Introduction

Many years have passed by since, delivering the Inaugural Lecture of the Irish Literary Society in London, I advocated as one of its chief aims the recasting into modern form and in literary English of the old Irish legends, preserving the atmosphere of the original tales as much as possible, but clearing them from repetitions, redundant expressions, idioms interesting in Irish but repellent in English, and, above all, from absurdities, such as the sensational fancy of the later editors and bards added to the simplicities of the original tales.

Long before I spoke of this, it had been done by P.W. Joyce in his OLD CELTIC ROMANCES, and by Standish O'Grady for the whole story of Cuchulain, but in this case with so large an imitation of the Homeric manner that the Celtic spirit of the story was in danger of being lost. This was the fault I had to find with that inspiring book,[3] but it was a fault which had its own attraction.

Since then, a number of writers have translated into literary English a host of the Irish tales, and have done this with a just reverence for their originals. Being, in nearly every case, Irish themselves, they have tried, with varying success, to make their readers realize the wild scenery of Ireland, her vital union with the sea and the great ocean to the West, those changing dramatic skies, that mystic weather, the wizard woods and streams which form the constant background of these stories; nor have they failed to allure their listeners to breathe the spiritual air of Ireland, to feel its pathetic, heroic, imaginative thrill.

They have largely succeeded in their effort. The Irish bardic tales have now become a part of English literature and belong not only to grown up persons interested in early poetry, in mythology and folk-customs, but to the children of Ireland and England. Our new imaginative stories are now told in nurseries, listened to at evening when the children assemble in the fire-light to hear tales from their parents, and eagerly read by boys at school. A fresh world of story-telling has been opened to the imagination of the young.

This could not have been done in the right way if it had not been for the previous work of Celtic scholars in Ireland, and particularly on the Continent, in France and Germany. Having mastered medieval Irish, they have translated with careful accuracy many of the ancient tales, omitting and changing nothing; they have edited them critically, collating and comparing them with one another, and with other forms of the same stories. We have now in English, French, and German the exact representation of the originals with exhaustive commentaries.

When this necessary work was finished—and it was absolutely necessary—it had two important results on all work of the kind Mr Rolleston has performed in this book—on the imaginative recasting and modernizing of the ancient tales. First, it made it lawful and easy for the modern artist—in sculpture, painting, poetry, or imaginative prose—to use the stories as he pleased in order to give pleasure to the modern world. It made it lawful because he could reply to those who objected that what he produced was not the real thing—"The real thing exists; you will find it, when you wish to see it, accurately and closely translated by critical and competent scholars. I refer you to the originals in the notes to this book. I have found the materials of my stories in these originals; and it is quite lawful for me, now that they have been reverently preserved, to use them as I please for the purpose of giving pleasure to the modern world—to make out of them fresh imaginative work, as the medieval writers did out of the original stories of Arthur and his men." This is the defence any re-caster of the ancient tales might make of the *lawfulness* of his work, and it is a just defence; having, above all, this use—that it leaves the imagination of the modern artist free, yet within recognized and ruling limits, to play in and around his subject.

One of those limits is the preservation, in any remodelling of the tales, of the Celtic atmosphere. To tell the Irish stories in the manner of Homer or Apuleius, in the manner of the Norse sagas, or in the manner of Malory, would be to lose their very nature, their soul, their nationality. We should no longer understand the men and women who fought and loved in Ireland, and whose characters were moulded by Irish surroundings, customs, thoughts, and passions. We should not see or feel the landscape of Ireland or its skies, the streams, the woods, the animals and birds, the mountain solitudes, as we feel and see them in the original tales. We should not hear, as we hear in their first form, the stormy seas between Scotland and Antrim, or the great waves which roar on the western isles, and beat on cliffs which still belong to another world than ours. The genius of Ireland would desert our work.

And it would be a vast pity to lose the Irish atmosphere in the telling of the Irish tales, because it is unique; not only distinct from that of the stories of other races, but from that of the other branches of the Celtic race. It differs from the atmosphere of the stories of Wales, of Brittany, of the Highlands and islands of Scotland. It is more purely Celtic, less mixed than any of them. A hundred touches in feeling, in ways of thought, in sensitiveness to beauty, in war and voyaging, and in ideals of life, separate it from that of the other Celtic races.

It is owing to the careful, accurate, and critical work of continental and Irish scholars on the manuscript materials of Irish Law, History, Bardic Tales, and Poetry; on customs, dress, furniture, architecture, ornament, on hunting and sailing; on the manners of men and women in war and peace, that the modern re-teller of the Irish tales is enabled to conserve the Irish atmosphere. And this conservation of the special Irish atmosphere is the second result which the work of the critical scholars has established. If the re-writer of the tales does not use the immense materials made ready to his hand for illustration, expansion, ornament and description in such a way that Ireland, and only Ireland, lives in his work from line to line, he is greatly to be blamed.

Mr Rolleston has fulfilled these conditions with the skill and the feeling of an artist. He has clung closely to his originals with an affectionate regard for their ancientry, their ardour and their distinction, and yet has, within this limit, used and modified them with a pleasant freedom. His love of Ireland has instilled into his representation of these tales a passion akin to that which gave them birth. We feel, as we read, how deep his sympathy has been with their intensity, their love of wild nature, their desire for beauty, their interest in humanity and in character, their savagery and their tenderness, their fairy magic and strange imaginations that suddenly surprise and charm. Whenever anything lovely emerges in the tale, he does not draw attention to it, but touches it with so artistic a pencil that its loveliness is enhanced. And he has put into English verse the Irish poems scattered through the tales with the skill and the temper of a poet. I hope his book will win what it deserves—the glad appreciation of old and young in England, and the gratitude of Ireland.

The stories told in this book belong to three distinct cycles of Irish story-telling. The first are mythological, and are concerned with the early races that are fabled to have dwelt and fought in Ireland Among these the Tuatha De Danaan were the final conquerors, and held the land for two hundred years They were, it is supposed, of the Celtic stock, but they were not the ancestors of the present Irish. These were the Milesians (Irish, Scots or Gaelic who, conquering the Tuatha De Danaan, ruled Ireland till they were overcome by the English.) The stories which have to do with the Tuatha De Danaan are mythical and of a great antiquity concerning men and women, the wisest and the best of whom became gods, and who appear as divine beings in the cycle of tales which follow after them They were always at war with a fierce and savage people called Fomorians, whom they finally defeated and the strife between them may mythically represent the ancient war between the good and evil principles in the world.

In the next cycle we draw nearer to history, and are in the world not of myth but of legend. It is possible that some true history may be hidden underneath its sagas, that some of its personages may be historical, but we cannot tell. The events are supposed to occur about the time of the birth of Christ, and seventeen hundred years after those of the mythical period. This is the cycle which collects its wars and sorrows and splendours around the dominating figure of Cuchulain, and is called the Heroic or the Red Branch or the Ultonian cycle. Several sagas tell of the birth, the life, and the death of Cuchulain, and among them is the longest and the most important—the Táin—the *Cattle Raid of Cooley*.

Others are concerned with the great King Conor mac Nessa, and the most known and beautiful of these is the sorrowful tale of Deirdré. There are many others of the various heroes and noble women who belonged to the courts of Conor and of his enemy Queen Maev of Connaght. The *Carving of mac Datho's Boar*, the story of *Etain and Midir*, and the *Vengeance of Mesgedra*, contained in this book belong to these miscellaneous tales unconnected with the main saga of Cuchulain.

The second cycle is linked to the first, not by history or race, but by the fact that the great personages in the first have now become the gods who intervene in the affairs of the wars and heroes of the second. They take part in them as the gods do in the Iliad and the Odyssey. Lugh, the Long-Handed, the great Counsellor of the Tuatha De Danaan, is now a god, and is the real father of Cuchulain, heals him of his wounds in the Battle of the Ford, warns him of his coming death, and receives him into the immortal land. The Morrigan, who descends from the first cycle, is now the goddess of war, and is at first the enemy and afterwards the lover of Cuchulain. Angus, The Dagda, Mananan the sea-god, enter not only into the sagas of the second cycle, but into those of the third, of the cycle of Finn. And all along to the very end of the stories, and down indeed to the present day, the Tuatha De Danaan appear in various forms, slowly lessening in dignity and power, until they end in the fairy folk in whom the Irish peasants still believe. They are alive and still powerful in the third—the Fenian—cycle of stories, some of which are contained and adorned in this book. In their continued presence is the only connexion which exists between the three cycles. No personages of the first save these of the gods appear in the Heroic cycle, none of the Heroic cycle appears in the Fenian cycle. Seventeen hundred years, according to Irish annalists, separate the first from the second, more than two hundred years separate the second from the beginning of the third.

The third cycle is called Fenian because its legends tell, for the most part, of the great deeds of the Féni or Fianna, who were the militia employed by the High King to support his supremacy, to keep Ireland in order, to defend the country from foreign invasion. They were, it seems, finally organized by Cormac mac Art, 227 A.D.(?) the grandson of Conn the Hundred Fighter. But they had loosely existed before in the time of Conn and his son Art, and like all mercenary bodies of this kind were sometimes at war with the kings who employed them. Finally, at the battle of Gowra, they and their power were quite destroyed. Long before this destruction, they were led in the reign of Cormac by Finn the son of Cumhal, and it is around Finn and Oisín the son of Finn, that most of the romances of the Fenian cycle are gathered. Others which tell of the battles and deeds of Conn and Art and Cormac and Cairbre of the Liffey, Cormac's son, are more or less linked on to the Fenians. On the whole, Finn and his warriors, each of a distinct character, warlike skill and renown, are the main personages of the cycle, and though Finn is not the greatest warrior, he is their head and master because he is the wisest; and this masterdom by knowledge is for the first time an element in Irish stories.

If the tales of the first cycle are mythological and of the second heroic, these are romantic. The gods have lost their dreadful, even their savage character, and have become the Fairies, full often of gentleness, grace, and humour. The mysterious dwelling places of the gods in the sea, in unknown lands, in the wandering air, are now in palaces under the green hills of Ireland, or by the banks of swift clear rivers, like the palace of Angus near the Boyne, or across the seas in Tir-na-n-Óg, the land of immortal youth,

7

whither Niam brings Oisín to live with her in love, as Morgan le Fay brought Ogier the Dane to her fairyland. The land of the Immortals in the heroic cycle, to which, in the story of *Etain and Midir* in this book, Midir brings back Etain after she has sojourned for a time on earth, is quite different in conception from the Land of Youth over the far seas where delightfulness of life and love is perfect. This, in its conception of an unknown world where is immortal youth, where stormless skies, happy hunting, strange adventure, gentle manners dwell, where love is free and time is unmarked, is pure romance. So are the adventures of Finn against enchanters, as in the story of the *Birth of Oisín*, of *Dermot in the Country under the Seas*, in the story of the *Pursuit of the Gilla Dacar*, of the wild love-tale of *Dermot and Grania*, flying for many years over all Ireland from the wrath of Finn, and of a host of other tales of enchantments and battle, and love, and hunting, and feasts, and discoveries, and journeys, invasions, courtships, and solemn mournings. No doubt the romantic atmosphere has been deepened in these tales by additions made to them by successive generations of bardic singers and storytellers, but for all that the original elements in the stories are romantic as they are not in the previous cycles.

Again, these Fenian tales are more popular than the others. Douglas Hyde has dwelt on this distinction. "For 1200 years at least, they have been," he says, "intimately bound up with the thought and feelings of the whole Gaelic race in Ireland and Scotland." Even at the present day new forms are given to the tales in the cottage homes of Ireland. And it is no wonder. The mysterious giant forms of the mythological period, removed by divinity from the sympathy of men; the vast heroic figures of Cuchulain and his fellows and foes, their close relation to supernatural beings and their doings, are far apart from the more natural humanity of Cormac and Finn, of Dermot and Goll, of Oisín and Oscar, of Keelta, and last of Conan, the coward, boaster and venomous tongue, whom all the Fenians mocked and yet endured. They are a very human band of fighting men, and though many of them, like Oisín and Finn and Dermot, have adventures in fairyland, they preserve in these their ordinary human nature. The Connacht peasant has no difficulty in following Finn into the cave of Slieve Cullinn, where the witch turned him into a withered old man, for the village where he lives has traditions of the same kind; the love affairs of Finn, of Dermot and Grania, and of many others, are quite in harmony with a hundred stories, and with the temper, of Irish lovers. A closer, a simpler humanity than that of the other cycles pervades the Fenian cycle, a greater chivalry, a greater courtesy, and a greater tenderness. We have left the primeval savagery behind, the multitudinous slaughtering, the crude passions of the earlier men and women; we are nearer to civilization, nearer to the common temper and character of the Irish people. No one can doubt this who will compare the *Vengeance of Mesgedra* with the *Chase of the Gilla Dacar*.

The elaborate courtesy with which Finn and his chief warriors receive all comers, as in the story of Vivionn the giantess, is quite new, even medieval in its chivalry; so is the elaborate code of honour; so also is, on the whole, the treatment of women and their relation to men. How far this resemblance to medieval romance has been intruded into the stories—(there are some in which there is not a trace of it)— by the after editors and re-editors of the tales, I cannot tell, but however that may be, their presence in the Fenian cycle is plain; and this brings the stories into a kindlier and more pleasurable atmosphere for modern readers than that which broods in thunderous skies and fierce light over dreadful passions and battles thick and bloody in the previous cycles. We are in a gentler world.

Another more modern romantic element in the Fenian legends is the delight in hunting, and that more affectionate relation of men to animals which always marks an advance in civilization. Hunting, as in medieval romance, is one of the chief pleasures of the Fenians. Six months of the year they passed in the open, getting to know every part of the country they had to defend, and hunting through the great woods and over the hills for their daily food and their daily delight. The story of the *Chase of the Gilla Dacar* tells, at its beginning, of a great hunting and of Finn's men listening with joy to the cries of the hunters and the loud chiding of the dogs; and many tales celebrate the following of the stag and the wild boar from early dawn to the evening. Then Finn's two great hounds, Bran and Sceolaun, are loved by Finn and his men as if they were dear friends; and they, when their master is in danger or under enchantment wail like human beings for his loss or pain. It is true Cuchulain's horses weep tears of blood when he goes forth to his last battle, foreknowing his death; but they are immortal steeds and have divine knowledge of fate. The dogs of Finn are only dogs, and the relation between him and them is a natural relation, quite unlike the relation between Cuchulain and the horses which draw his chariot. Yet Finn's dogs are not quite as other dogs. They have something of a human soul in them. They know that in the milk-white fawn they pursue there is an enchanted maiden, and they defend her from the other hounds till Finn arrives. And it is told of them that sometimes, when the moon is high, they rise from their graves and meet and hunt together, and speak of ancient days. The supernatural has lessened since the heroic cycle. But it is still there in the Fenian.

Again, the Fenian cycle of tales is more influenced by Christianity than the others are. The mythological cycle is not only fully pagan, it is primeval. It has the vastness, the savagery, the relentlessness of nature-myths, and what beauty there is in it is akin to terror. Gentleness is unknown. There is only one exception to this, so far as I know, and that is in the story of *The Children of Lir*. It is plain, however, that the Christian ending of that sorrowful story is a later addition to it. It is remarkably well done, and most tenderly. I believe that the artist who did it imported into the rest of the tale the exquisite tenderness which fills it, and yet with so much reverence for his original that he did not make the body of the story Christian. He kept the definite Christian element to the very end, but he filled the whole with its tender atmosphere.

No Christianity and very little gentleness intrude into the heroic cycle. The story of Christ once touches it, but he who put it in did not lose the pagan atmosphere, or the wild fierceness of the manners of the time. How it was done may be read in this book at the end of the story of the *Vengeance of Mesgedra*. Very late in the redaction of these stories a Christian tag was also added to the tale of the death of Cuchulain, but it was very badly done.

When we come to the Fenian cycle there is a well-defined borderland between them and Christianity. The bulk of the stories is plainly pagan; their originals were frankly so. But the temper of their composers is more civilized than that of those who conceived the tales of the previous cycles; the manners, as I have already said, of their personages are gentler, more chivalrous; and their atmosphere is so much nearer to that of Christianity, that the new Christian elements would find themselves more at home in them than in the terrible vengeance of Lugh, the savage brutality of Conor to Deirdré, or the raging slaughterings of Cuchulain. So much was this the case that a story was skilfully invented which linked in imagination the Fenian cycle to a Christianized Ireland. This story—*Oisín in the Land of Youth*—is contained in this book. Oisín, or Ossian, the son of Finn, in an enchanted story, lives for 300 years, always young, with his love in Tir-na-n-Óg, and finds on his return, when he becomes a withered old man, St Patrick and Christianity in Ireland. He tells to Patrick many tales of the Fenian wars and loves and glories, and in the course of them paganism and Christianity are contrasted and intermingled. A certain sympathy with the pagan ideas of honour and courage and love enters into the talk of Patrick and the monks, and softens their pious austerity. On the other hand, the Fenian legends are gentled and influenced by the Christian elements, in spite of the scorn with which Oisín treats the rigid condemnation of his companions and of Finn to the Christian hell, and the ascetic and unwarlike life of the monks.[4] There was evidently in the Fenian cycle of story-telling a transition period in which the bards ran Christianity and paganism in and out of one another, and mingled the atmosphere of both, and to that period the last editing of the story of *Lir and his Children* may be referred. A lovely story in this book, put into fine form by Mr Rolleston, is as it were an image of this transition time—the story or *How Ethne quitted Fairyland*. It takes us back to the most ancient cycle, for it tells of the great gods Angus and Mananan, and then of how they became, after their conquest by the race who live in the second cycle, the invisible dwellers in a Fairy country of their own during the Fenian period, and, afterwards, when Patrick and the monks had overcome paganism. Thus it mingles together elements from all the periods. The mention of the great caldron and the swine which always renew their food is purely mythological. The cows which come from the Holy Land are Christian. Ethne herself is born in the house of a pagan god who has become a Fairy King, but loses her fairy nature and becomes human; and the reason given for this is an interesting piece of psychology which would never have occurred to a pagan world. She herself is a transition maiden, and, suddenly finding herself outside the fairy world and lost, happens on a monastery and dies on the breast of St Patrick. But she dies because of the wild wailing for her loss of the fairy-host, whom she can hear but cannot see, calling to her out of the darkened sky to come back to her home. And in her sorrow and the battle in her between the love of Christ and of Faerie, she dies. That is a symbol, not intended as such by its conceiver, but all the more significant, of the transition time. Short as it is, few tales, perhaps, are more deeply charged with spiritual meaning.

Independent of these three cycles, but often touching them here and there, and borrowing from them, there are a number of miscellaneous tales which range from the earliest times till the coming of the Danes. The most celebrated of these are the *Storming of the Hostel* with the death of Conary the High King of Ireland, and the story of the Boru tribute. Two examples of these miscellaneous tales of a high antiquity are contained in this book—*King Iubdan and King Fergus* and *Etain and Midir*. Both of them have great charm and delightfulness.

Finally, the manner in which these tales grew into form must be remembered when we read them. At first, they were not written down, but recited in hall and with a harp's accompaniment by the various bardic story-tellers who were attached to the court of the chieftain, or wandered singing and reciting from court to court. Each bard, if he was a creator, filled up the original framework of the tale with ornaments of his own, or added new events or personages to the tale, or mixed it up with other related tales, or made new tales altogether attached to the main personages of the original tale—episodes in their lives into which the bardic fancy wandered. If these new forms of the tales or episodes were imaginatively true to the characters round which they were conceived and to the atmosphere of the time, they were taken up by other bards and became often separate tales, or if a great number attached themselves to one hero, they finally formed themselves into one heroic story, such as that which is gathered round Cuchulain, which, as it stands, is only narrative, but might in time have become epical. Indeed, the Tàin approaches, though at some distance, an epic. In this way that mingling of elements out of the three cycles into a single Saga took place.

Then when Christianity came, the Irish who always, Christians or not, loved their race and its stories, would not let them go. They took them and suffused them with a Christian tenderness, even a Christian forgiveness. Or they inserted Christian endings, while they left the rest of the stories as pagan as before. Later on, while the stories were still learned by the bards and recited, they were written down, and somewhat spoiled by a luxurious use of ornamental adjectives, and by the weak, roving and uninventive fancy of men and monks aspiring to literature but incapable of reaching it.

However, in spite of all this intermingling and of the different forms of the same story, it is possible for an intelligent and sensitive criticism, well informed in comparative mythology and folklore, to isolate what is very old in these tales from that which is less old, and that in turn from that which is still less old, and that from what is partly historical, medieval or modern. This has been done, with endless controversy, by those excellent German, French, and Irish scholars who have, with a thirsty pleasure, recreated the ancient literature of Ireland, and given her once more a literary name among the nations—a name which, having risen again, will not lose but increase its brightness.

As to the stories themselves, they have certain well-marked characteristics, and in dwelling on these, I shall chiefly refer, for illustration, to the stories in this book. Some of these characteristic elements belong to almost all mythological tales, and arise from human imagination, in separated lands, working in the same or in a similar way on the doings of Nature, and impersonating them. The form, however, in which these original ideas are cast is, in each people, modified and varied by the animal life, the climate, the configuration of the country, the nearness of mountain ranges and of the sea, the existence of wide forests or vast plains, of swift rivers and great inland waters.

The earliest tales of Ireland are crowded with the sea that wrapt the island in its arms; and on the west and north the sea was the mighty and mysterious Ocean, in whose far infinities lay for the Irish the land of Immortal Youth. Between its shining shores and Ireland, strange islands—dwelt in by dreadful or by fair and gracious creatures, whose wonders Maeldun and Brendan visited—lay like jewels on the green and sapphire waters. Out of this vast ocean emerged also their fiercest enemies. Thither, beyond these islands into the Unknown, over the waves on a fairy steed, went Oisín with Niam; thither, in after years, sailed St Brendan, till it seemed he touched America. In the ocean depths were fair cities and well-grassed lands and cattle, which voyagers saw through water thin and clear. There, too, Brian, one of the sons of Turenn, descended in his water-dress and his crystal helmet, and found high-bosomed maidens weaving in a shining hall. Into the land beneath the wave, Mananan, the proud god of the sea brought Dermot and Finn and the Fianna to help him in his wars, as is told in the story of the *Gilla Dacar*. On these western seas, near the land, Lir's daughters, singing and floating, passed three hundred years. On other seas, in the storm and in the freezing sleet that trouble the dark waves of Moyle, between Antrim and the Scottish isles, they spent another three centuries. Half the story of the Sons of Usnach has to do with the crossing of seas and with the coast. Even Cuchulain, who is a land hero, in one of the versions of his death, dies fighting the sea-waves. The sound, the restlessness, the calm, the savour and the infinite of the sea, live in a host of these stories; and to cap all, the sea itself and Mananan its god sympathise with the fates of Erin. When great trouble threatens Ireland, or one of her heroes is near death, there are three huge waves which, at three different points, rise, roaring, out of the ocean, and roll, flooding every creek and bay and cave and river round the whole coast with tidings of sorrow and doom. Later on, in the Fenian tales, the sea is not so prominent. Finn and his clan are more concerned with the land. Their work, their hunting and adventures carry them over the mountains and plains, through the forests, and by the lakes and rivers. In the stories there is scarcely any part of Ireland which is not linked, almost geographically, with its scenery. Even the ancient gods have retired from the coast to live in the pleasant green hills or by the wooded shores of the great lakes or in hearing of the soft murmur of the rivers. This business of the sea, this varied aspect of the land, crept into the imagination of the Irish, and were used by them to embroider and adorn their poems and tales. They do not care as much for the doings of the sky. There does not seem to be any supreme god of the heaven in their mythology. Neither the sun nor the moon are specially worshipped. There are sun-heroes like Lugh, but no isolated sun-god. The great beauty of the cloud-tragedies of storm, the gorgeous sunrises and sunsets, so dramatic in Ireland, or the magnificence of the starry heavens, are scarcely celebrated. But the Irish folk have heard the sound of the wind in the tree-tops and marked its cold swiftness over the moor, and watched with fear or love the mists of ocean and the bewilderment of the storm-driven snow and the sweet falling of the dew. These are fully celebrated.

These great and small aspects of Nature are not only celebrated, they are loved. One cannot read the stories in this book without feeling that the people who conceived and made them observed Nature and her ways with a careful affection, which seems to be more developed in the Celtic folk than elsewhere in modern Europe. There is nothing which resembles it in Teutonic story-telling. In the story of *The Children of Lir*, though there is no set description of scenery, we feel the spirit of the landscape by the lake where Lir listened for three hundred years to the sweet songs of his children. And, as we read of their future fate, we are filled with the solitude and mystery, the ruthlessness and beauty of the ocean. Even its gentleness on quiet days enters from the tale into our imagination. Then, too, the mountain-glory and the mountain-gloom are again and again imaginatively described and loved. The windings and recesses, the darkness and brightness of the woods and the glades therein, enchant the Fenians even when they are in mortal danger. And the waters of the great lakes, the deep pools of the rivers, the rippling shallows, the green banks, the brown rushing of the torrents, are all alive in the prose and song of Ireland. How deep was the Irish love of these delightful things is plain from their belief that "the place of the revealing of poetry was always by the margin of water." And the Salmon of Knowledge, the eating of which gave Finn his pre-eminence, swam in a green pool, still and deep, over which hung a rowan tree that shed its red berries on the stream. Lovely were the places whence Art and Knowledge came.

Then, as to all good landscape lovers, the beasts, birds, and insects of Nature were dear to these ancient people. One of the things Finn most cared for was not only his hounds, but the "blackbird singing on Letterlee"; and his song, on page 114, in the praise of May, tells us how keen was his observant eye for animal life and how much it delighted him. The same minute realisation of natural objects is illustrated in this book when King Iubdan explains to the servant the different characteristics of the trees of the forest, and the mystic elements that abide in them. It was a habit, even of Teutonic poets, to tell of the various trees and their uses in verse, and Spenser and Drayton have both done it in later times. But few of them have added, as the Irish story does, a spiritual element to their description, and made us think of malign or beneficent elements attached to them. The woodbine, and this is a strange fancy, is the king of the woods. The rowan is the tree of the magicians, and its berries are for poets. The bramble is inimical to man, the alder is full of witchcraft, and the elder is the wood of the horses of the fairies. Into every tree a spiritual power is infused; and the good lords of the forest are loved of men and birds and bees.

Thus the Irish love of nature led them to spiritualise, in another way than mythical, certain things in nature, and afterwards to humanise, up to a certain point, the noble implements wrought by human skill out of natural materials. And this is another element in all these stories, as it is in the folk-lore also of other lands. In the tale of the Sons of Turenn, the stones of the wayside tell to Lugh the story of the death of his father Kian, and the boat of Mananan, indwelt by a spirit, flies hither and thither over the seas, obeying the commands, even the thought, of its steersman. The soul of some famed spears is so hot for slaughter that, when it is not being used in battle, its point must stand in a bath of blood or of drowsy herbs, lest it should slay the host. The swords murmur and hiss and cry out for the battle; the shield of the hero hums louder and louder, vibrating for the encouragement of the warrior. Even the wheels of Cuchulain's chariot roar as they whirl into the fight. This partial life given to the weapons of war is not specially Celtic. Indeed, it is more common in Teutonic than in Celtic legend, and it seems probable that it was owing to the Norsemen that it was established in the Hero tales of Ireland.

This addition of life, or of some of the powers of life, to tree and well and boulder-stone, to river and lake and hill, and sword and spear, is common to all mythologies, but the special character of each nation or tribe modifies the form of the life-imputing stories. In Ireland the tree, the stream were not dwelt in by a separate living being, as in Grecian story; the half-living powers they had were given to them from without, by the gods, the demons, the fairies; and in the case of the weapons, the powers they had of act or sound arose from the impassioned thoughts and fierce emotions of their forger or their wielder, which, being intense, were magically transferred to them. The Celtic nature is too fond of reality, too impatient of illusion, to believe in an actual living spirit in inanimate things. At least, that is the case in the stories of the Hero and the Fenian Cycles.[5]

What the Irish of the Heroic, and still more of the Fenian Cycle, did make in their imagination was a world, outside of themselves, of living spiritual beings, in whose actuality they fully believed, and in whom a great number of them still believe. A nation, if I may use this term, dwelt under the sea. Another dwelt in the far island of the ocean, the Isle of the Ever-Young. Another dwelt in the land, in the green hills and by the streams of Ireland; and these were the ancient gods who had now lost their dominion over the country, but lived on, with all their courtiers and warriors and beautiful women in a country underground. As time went on, their powers were dwarfed, and they became small of size, less beautiful, and in our modern times are less inclined to enter into the lives of men and women. But the Irish peasant still sees them flitting by his path in the evening light, or dancing on the meadow round the grassy mound, singing and playing strange melodies; or mourns for the child they have carried away to live with them and forget her people, or watches with fear his dreaming daughter who has been touched by them, and is never again quite a child of this earth, or quite of the common race of man.

These were the invisible lands and peoples of the Irish imagination; and they live in and out of many of the stories. Cuchulain is lured into a fairy-land, and lives for more than a year in love with Fand, Mananan's wife. Into another fairy-land, through zones of mist, Cormac, as is told here, was lured by Mananan, who now has left the sea to play on the land. Oisín, as I have already said, flies with Niam over the sea to the island of Eternal Youth. Etain, out of the immortal land, is born into an Irish girl and reclaimed and carried back to her native shore by Midir, a prince of the Fairy Host. Ethne, whose story also is here, has lived for all her youth in the court of Angus, deep in the hill beside the rushing of the Boyne.

These stories are but a few out of a great number of the loves and wars between the men and women of the human and the fairy races. Curiously enough, as the stories become less ancient, the relations between men and the fairies are more real, more close, even more affectionate. Finn and the Fianna seem to be almost in daily companionship with the fairy host—much nearer to them than the men of the Heroic Cycle are to the gods. They interchange love and music and battle and adventure with one another. They are, for the most part, excellent friends; and their intercourse suffers from no doubt. It is as real as the intercourse between Welsh and English on the Borderland.

There was nothing illusive, nothing merely imaginary, in these fairy worlds for the Irish hero or the Irish people. They believed the lands to be as real as their own, and the indwellers of fairyland to have like passions with themselves. Finn is not a bit surprised when Vivionn the giantess sits beside him on the hill, or Fergus when King Iubdan stands on his hand; or St Patrick when Ethne, out of fairyland, dies on his breast, or when he sees, at his spell, Cuchulain, dead some nine hundred years, come forth out of the dark gates of Sheol, high in his chariot, grasping his deadly spear, driven as of old by his well-loved charioteer, drawn by the immortal steeds through the mist, and finally talking of his deeds and claiming a place in the Christian heaven—a place that Patrick yields to him. The invisible worlds lived, loved, and thought around this visible world, and were, it seems, closer and more real to the Celtic than to other races.

But it was not only these agreeable and lovely folk in pleasant habitations whom the Irish made, but also spirits of another sort, of lesser powers and those chiefly malignant, having no fixed dwelling-place, homeless in the air and drifting with it, embodying the venomous and deadly elements of the earth and the angers and cruelty of the sea, and the hypocrisy of them all—demons, some of whom, like the stepmother of the children of Lir, have been changed from men or women because of wicked doings, but the most part born of the evil in Nature herself. They do what harm they can to innocent folk; they enter into, support, and direct—like Macbeth's witches—the evil thoughts of men; they rejoice in the battle, in the wounds and pain and death of men; they shriek and scream and laugh around the head of the hero when he goes forth, like Cuchulain, to an unwearied slaughter of men. They make the blight, the deadly mist, the cruel tempest. To deceive is their pleasure; to discourage, to baffle, to ruin the hero is their happiness. Some of them are monsters of terrific aspect who abide in lakes or in desolate rocks, as the terrible tri-formed horse whom Fergus mac Leda conquered and by whom he died.

Naturally, as a link between these supernatural worlds and the natural world, there arose a body of men and women in Irish legend who, by years of study, gained a knowledge of, and power over, the supernatural beings, and used these powers for hurt to the enemies of their kingdom, or for help to their own people. Some were wise, learned, and statesmanlike, and used their powers for good. These were the high Druids, and every king had a band of them at his court and in his wars. They practiced what the Middle Ages called white magic. Others were wizards, magicians, witches, who, like the children of Cailitin, the foes of Cuchulain, or the three mutilated women whom Maev educated in evil craft to do evil to her foes, or the dread band that deceived Cuchulain into his last ride of death, practised black magic— evil, and the ministers of evil. Magic, and the doing of it, runs through the whole of Irish story-telling, and not only into pagan but also into Christian legend; for it was easy to change the old gods into devils, to keep the demonic creatures as demons, to replace the wise Druids by the priests and saints, and the wizards by the heretics who gave themselves to sorcery. Thus the ancient supernaturalism of the Irish has continued, with modern modifications, to the present day. The body of thought is much the same as it was in the days of Conor and Finn; the clothing is a bit different.

Another characteristic of the stories, especially in the mythological period, is the barbaric brutality which appears in them. Curiously mingled with this, in direct contrast, is their tenderness. These extreme contrasts are common in the Celtic nature. A Gael, whether of Ireland or the Western Isles, will pass in a short time from the wildest spirits, dancing and singing and drinking, into deep and grim depression—the child of the present, whether in love or war; and in the tales of Ireland there is a similar contrast between their brutality and their tenderness. The sudden fierce jealousy and the pitiless cruelty of their stepmother to the children of Lir is set over against the exquisite tenderness of Fionnuala, which pervades the story like an air from heaven. The noble tenderness of Deirdre, of Naisi and his brothers, in life and death, to one another, is lovelier in contrast with the savage and treacherous revenge of Conor. The great pitifulness of Cuchulain's fight with his dear friend Ferdia, whom he is compelled to slay; the crowning tenderness of Emer's recollective love in song before she dies on Cuchulain's dead body, are in full contrast with the savage hard-heartedness and cruelties of Maev, and with the ruthless slaughters Cuchulain made of his foes, out of which he seems often to pass, as it were, in a moment, into tenderness and gracious speech. Even Finn, false for once to his constant courtesy, revenges himself on Dermot so pitilessly that both his son and grandson cry shame upon him.

Of course this barbaric cruelty is common to all early periods in every nation; and, whenever fierce passion is aroused, to civilised nations also. What is remarkable in the Irish tales is the contemporary tenderness. The Vikings were as savage as the Irish, but the savagery is not mingled with the Irish tenderness. At last, when we pass from the Hero Cycle into the Cycle of Finn, there is scarcely any of the ancient brutality to be found in the host of romantic stories which gather round the chivalry of the Fenians.

There are other characteristics of these old tales on which I must dwell. The first is the extra-ordinary love of colour. This is not a characteristic of the early German, English or Scandinavian poems and tales. Its remarkable presence in Scottish poetry, at a time when it is scarcely to be found in English literature, I have traced elsewhere to the large admixture of Celtic blood in the Lowlands of Scotland. In early Irish work it is to be found everywhere. In descriptions of Nature, which chiefly appear in the Fenian Cycle and in Christian times, colour is not as much dwelt on as we should expect, for nowhere that I have seen is it more delicate and varied than under the Irish atmosphere. Yet, again and again, the amber colour of the streams as they come from the boglands, and the crimson and gold of the sunsetting, and the changing green of the trees, and the blue as it varies and settles down on the mountains when they go to their rest, and the green crystal of the sea in calm and the dark purple of it in storm, and the white foam of the waves when they grow black in the squall, and the brown of the moors, and the yellow and rose and crimson of the flowers, and many another interchanging of colour, are seen and spoken of as if it were a common thing always to dwell on colour. This literary custom I do not find in any other Western literature. It is even more remarkable in the descriptions of the dress and weapons of the warriors and kings. They blaze with colour; and as gold was plentiful in Ireland in those far-off days, yellow and red are continually flashing in and out of the blue and green and rich purple of their dress. The women are dressed in as rich colours as the men. When Eochy met Etain by the spring of pure water, as told in this book, she must have flashed in the sunlight like a great jewel. Then, the halls where they met and the houses of the kings are represented as glorious with colour, painted in rich patterns, hung with woven cloths dyed deep with crimson and blue and green and yellow. The common things in use, eating and drinking implements, the bags they carry, the bed-clothing, the chess-men, the tables, are embroidered or chased or set with red carbuncles or white stones or with interlacing of gold. Colour is everywhere and everywhere loved. And where colour is loved the arts flourish, as the decorative arts flourished in Ireland.

Lastly, on this matter, the Irish tale-tellers, even to the present day, dwell with persistence on the colour of the human body as a special loveliness, and with as much love of it as any Venetian when he painted it. And they did this with a comparison of its colour to the colours they observed in Nature, so that the colour of one was harmonised with the colour of the other. I might quote many such descriptions of the appearance of the warriors—they are multitudinous—but the picture of Etain is enough to illustrate what I say—"Her hair before she loosed it was done in two long tresses, yellow like the flower of the waterflag in summer or like red gold. Her hands were white as the snow of a single night, and her eyes as blue as the dark hyacinth, and her lips red as the berries of the rowan-tree, and her body as white as the foam of the sea-waves. The radiance of the moon was in her face and the light of wooing in her eyes." So much for the Irish love of colour.[6]

Their love of music was equally great; and was also connected with Nature. "The sound of the flowing of streams." said one of their bardic clan, "is sweeter than any music of men." "The harp of the woods is playing music," said another. In Finn's Song to May, the waterfall is singing a welcome to the pool below, the loudness of music is around the hill, and in the green fields the stream is singing. The blackbird, the cuckoo, the heron and the lark are the musicians of the world. When Finn asks his men what music they thought the best, each says his say, but Oisín answers, "The music of the woods is sweetest to me, the sound of the wind and of the blackbird, and the cuckoo and the soft silence of the heron." And Finn himself, when asked what was his most beloved music, said first that it was "the sharp whistling of the wind as it went through the uplifted spears of the seven battalions of the Fianna," and this was fitting for a hero to say. But when the poet in him spoke, he said his music was the crying of the sea-gull, and the noise of the waves, and the voice of the cuckoo when summer was at hand, and the washing of the sea against the shore, and of the tide when it met the river of the White Trout, and of the wind rushing through the cloud. And many other sayings of the same kind this charming and poetic folk has said concerning those sweet, strong sounds in Nature out of which the music of men was born.

Again, there is not much music in the Mythological Tales. Lugh, it is true, is a great harper, and the harp of the Dagda, into which he has bound his music, plays a music at whose sound all men laugh, and another so that all men weep, and another so enthralling that all fall asleep; and these three kinds of music are heard through all the Cycles of Tales. Yet when the old gods of the mythology became the Sidhe,[7] the Fairy Host, they—having left their barbaric life behind—became great musicians. In every green hill where the tribes of fairy-land lived, sweet, wonderful music was heard all day—such music that no man could hear but he would leave all other music to listen to it, which "had in it sorrows that man has never felt, and joys for which man has no name, and it seemed as if he who heard it might break from time into eternity and be one of the immortals." And when Finn and his people lived, they, being in great harmony and union with the Sidhe, heard in many adventures with them their lovely music, and it became their own. Indeed, Finn, who had twelve musicians, had as their chief one of the Fairy Host who came to dwell with him, a little man who played airs so divine that all weariness and sorrow fled away. And from him Finn's musicians learnt a more enchanted art than they had known before. And so it came to pass that as in every fairy dwelling there was this divine art, so in every palace and chieftain's hall, and in every farm, there were harpers harping on their harps, and all the land was full of sweet sounds and airs—shaping in music, imaginative war, and sorrows, and joys, and aspiration. Nor has their music failed. Still in the west and south of Ireland, the peasant, returning home, hears, as the evening falls from the haunted hills, airs unknown before, or at midnight a wild triumphant song from the Fairy Host rushing by, or wakes with a dream melody in his heart. And these are played and sung next day to the folk sitting round the fire. Many who heard these mystic sounds became themselves the makers of melodies, and went about the land singing and making and playing from village to village and cabin to cabin, till the unwritten songs of Ireland were as numerous as they were various. Moore collected a hundred and twenty of them, but of late more than five hundred he knew not of have been secured from the people and from manuscripts for the pleasure of the world. And in them lives on the spirit of the Fianna, and the mystery of the Fairy Host, and the long sorrow and the fleeting joy of the wild weather in the heart of the Irish race.

As to the poetry of Ireland, that other Art which is illustrated in this book, so fully has it been dwelt on by many scholars and critics that it needs not be touched here other than lightly and briefly. The honour and dignity of the art of poetry goes back in Irish mythology to a dim antiquity. The ancient myth said that the nine hazels of wisdom grew round a deep spring beneath the sea, and the hazels were the hazels of inspiration and of poetry—so early in Ireland were inspiration and poetry made identical with wisdom. Seven streams of wisdom flowed from that fountain-head, and when they had fed the world returned to it again. And all the art-makers of mankind, and of all arts, have drunk of their waters. Five salmon in the spring ate of the hazel nuts, and some haunted the rivers of Ireland; and whosoever, like Finn, tasted the flesh of these immortal fish, was possessed of the wisdom which is inspiration and poetry. Such was the ancient Irish conception of the art of poetry.

It is always an art which grows slowly into any excellence, and it needs for such growth a quieter life than the Irish lived for many centuries. Poems appear but rarely in the mythological or heroic cycles, and are loosely scattered among the prose of the bardic tales. A few are of war, but they are chiefly dirges like the Song of Emer over the dead body of Cuchulain, or that of Deirdre over Naisi—pathetic wailings for lost love. There is an abrupt and pitiful pain in the brief songs of Fionnuala, but I fancy these were made and inserted in Christian times. Poetry was more at home among the Fianna. The conditions of life were easier; there was more leisure and more romance. And the other arts, which stimulate poetry, were more widely practised than in the earlier ages. Finn's Song to May, here translated, is of a good type, frank and observant, with a fresh air in it, and a fresh pleasure in its writing. I have no doubt that at this time began the lyric poetry of Ireland, and it reached, under Christian influences, a level of good, I can scarcely say excellent, work, at a time when no other lyrical poetry in any vernacular existed in Europe or the Islands. It was religious, mystic, and chiefly pathetic—prayers, hymns, dirges, regrets in exile, occasional stories of the saints whose legendary acts were mixed with pagan elements, and most of these were adorned with illustrations drawn from natural beauty or from the doings of birds and beasts—a great affection for whom is prominent in the Celtic nature. The Irish poets sent this lyric impulse into Iceland, Wales, and Scotland, and from Scotland into England; and the rise of English vernacular poetry instead of Latin in the seventh and eighth centuries is due to the impulse given by the Irish monasteries at Whitby and elsewhere in Northumbria. The first rude lyric songs of Cædmon were probably modelled on the hymns of Colman.

One would think that poetry, which arose so early in a nation's life, would have developed fully. But this was not the case in Ireland. No narrative, dramatic, didactic, or epic poetry of any importance arose, and many questions and answers might be made concerning this curious restriction of development. The most probable solution of this problem is that there was never enough peace in Ireland or continuity of national existence or unity, to allow of a continuous development of any one of the arts into all its forms. Irish poetry never advanced beyond the lyric. In that form it lasted all through the centuries; it lasts still at the present day, and Douglas Hyde has proved how much charm belongs to it in his book on the *Love Songs of Connacht*.

It has had a long, long history; it has passed through many phases; it has sung of love and sorrow, of national wars and hopes, of Ireland herself as the Queen of Sorrow, of exile regrets from alien shores, of rebellion, of hatred of England, of political strife, in ballads sung in the streets, of a thousand issues of daily life and death—but of world-wide affairs, of great passions and duties and fates evolving in epic or clashing in drama, of continuous human lives in narrative (except in prose), of the social life of cities or of philosophic thought enshrined in stately verse, it has not sung. What it may do in the future, if Irish again becomes a tongue of literature in lofty poetry, lies on the knees of the gods. I wish it well, but such a development seems now too late. The Irish genius, if it is to speak in drama, in narrative poetry or in an epic, must speak, if it is to influence or to charm the world beyond the Irish shore, in a world-language like English, and of international as well as of Irish humanity.

These elements on which I have dwelt seem to me the most distinctive, the most Irish, in the Tales in this book. There are many others on which a more minute analysis might exercise itself, phases of feeling concerning war or love or friendship or honour or the passions, but these are not specially Irish. They belong to common human nature, and have their close analogies in other mythologies, in other Folk-tales, in other Sagas. I need not touch them here. But there is one element in all the Irish tales which I have not yet mentioned, and it brings all the others within its own circumference, and suffuses them with its own atmosphere. It is the love of Ireland, of the land itself for its own sake—a mystic, spiritual imaginative passion which in the soul of the dweller in the country is a constant joy, and in the heart of the exile is a sick yearning for return. There are not many direct expressions of this in the stories; but it underlies the whole of them, and it is also in the air they breathe. But now and again it does find clear expression, and in each of the cycles we have discussed. When the sons of Turenn are returning, wounded to death, from the Hill of Mochaen, they felt but one desire. "Let us but see," said Iuchar and Iucharba to their brother Brian, "the land of Erin again, the hills round Telltown, and the dewy plain of Bregia and the quiet waters of the Boyne and our father's Dún thereby, and healing will come to us; or if death come, we can endure it after that." Then Brian raised them up; and they saw that they were now near by under Ben Edar; and at the strand of the Bull they came to land. That is from the Mythological Cycle.

In the Heroic Cycle it appears in the longing cry for return to Ireland of Naisi and his brothers, which drives them out of Alba to their death; but otherwise it is rarely expressed. In the Fenian Cycle it exists, not in any clear words, but in a general delight in the rivers, lakes, woods, valleys, plains, and mountains of Ireland. Every description of them, and of life among them, is done with a loving, observant touch; and moreover, the veil of magic charm is thrown over all the land by the creation in it of the life and indwelling of the fairy host. The Fianna loved their country well.

When Christianity came, this deep-set sentiment did not lessen. It grew even stronger, and in exile it became a passion. It is illustrated by the songs of deep regret and affection Columba made in Iona, from whose rocky shores he looked day after day towards the west while the mists rose over Ireland. One little story of great beauty enshrines his passion. One morning he called to his side one of his monks, and said, "Go to the margin of the sea on the western side of our isle; and there, coming from the north of Ireland, you will see a voyaging crane, very weary and beaten by the storms, and it will fall at your feet on the beach. Lift it up with pity and carry it to the hut, nourish it for three days, and when it is refreshed and strong again it will care no more to stay with us in exile, but to fly back to sweet Ireland, the dear country where it was born. I charge you thus, for it comes from the land where I was born myself." And when his servant returned, having done as he was ordered, Columba said, "May God bless you, my son. Since you have well cared for our exiled guest, you will see it return to its own land in three days." And so it was. It rose, sought its path for a moment through the sky, and took flight on a steady wing for Ireland. The spirit of that story has never died in the soul of the Irish and in their poetry up to the present day.

Lastly, as we read these stories, even in a modern dress, an impression of great ancientry is made upon us, so much so that some scholars have tried to turn Finn into a mythical hero—but if he be as old as that implies, of how great an age must be the clearly mythic tales which gather round the Tuatha de Danaan? However this may be, the impression of ancientry is deep and agreeable. All myths in any nation are, of course, of a high antiquity, but as they treat of the beginning of things, they mingle an impression of youth with one of age. This is very pleasant to the imagination, and especially so if the myths, as in Ireland, have some poetic beauty or strangeness, as in the myth I have referred to—of the deep spring of clear water and the nine hazels of wisdom that encompass it. This mingling of the beauty of youth and the honour of ancientry runs through all the Irish tales. Youth and the love of it, of its beauty and strength, adorn and vitalize their grey antiquity. But where, in their narrative, the hero's youth is over and the sword weak in his hand, and the passion less in his and his sweetheart's blood, life is represented as scarcely worth the living. The famed men and women die young—the sons of Turenn, Cuchulain, Conall, Dermot, Emer, Deirdre, Naisi, Oscar. Oisín has three hundred years of youth in that far land in the invention of which the Irish embodied their admiration of love and youth. His old age, when sudden feebleness overwhelms him, is made by the bardic clan as miserable, as desolate as his youth was joyous. Again, Finn lives to be an old man, but the immortal was in him, and either he has been born again in several re-incarnations (for the Irish held from time to time the doctrine of the transmigration of souls), or he sleeps, like Barbarossa, in a secret cavern, with all his men around him, and beside him the mighty horn of the Fianna, which, when the day of fate and freedom comes, will awaken with three loud blasts the heroes and send them forth to victory. Old as she is, Ireland does not grow old, for she has never reached her maturity. Her full existence is before her, not behind her. And when she reaches it her ancientry and all its tales will be dearer to her than they have been in the past. They will be an inspiring national asset. In them and in their strange admixture of different and successive periods of customs, thoughts and emotions (caused by the continuous editing and re-editing of them, first in oral recitation and then at the hands of scribes), Ireland will see the record of her history, not the history of external facts, but of her soul as it grew into consciousness of personality; as it established in itself love of law, of moral right, of religion, of chivalry, of courtesy in war and daily life; as it rejoiced, and above all, as it suffered and was constant, in suffering and oppression, to its national ideals.

It seems as if, once at least, this aspect of the tales of Ireland was seen by men of old, for there is a story which tells that heaven itself desired their remembrance, and that we should be diverted and inspired by them. In itself it is a record of the gentleness of Irish Christianity to Irish heathendom, and of its love of the heroic past. For one day when Patrick and his clerks were singing the Mass at the Rath of the Red Ridge, where Finn was wont to be, he saw Keelta, a chief of the Fianna, draw near with his companions, and Keelta's huge hounds were with him. They were men so tall and great that fear fell on the clerks, but Patrick met with and asked their chieftain's name. "I am Keelta," he answered, "son of Ronan of the Fianna." "Was it not a good lord you were with," said Patrick, "Finn, son of Cumhal?" And Keelta said, "If the brown leaves falling in the wood were gold, if the waves of the sea were silver, Finn would have given them all away." "What was it kept you through your lifetime?" said Patrick. "Truth that was in our hearts, and strength in our hands, and fulfilment in our tongues," said Keelta. Then Patrick gave them food and drink and good treatment, and talked with them. And in the morning the two angels who guarded him came to him, and he asked them if it were any harm before God, King of heaven and earth, that he should listen to the stories of the Fianna. And the angels answered, "Holy Clerk, these old fighting men do not remember more than a third of their tales by reason of the forgetfulness of age, but whatever they tell write it down on the boards of the poets and in the words of the poets, for it will be a diversion to the companies and the high people of the latter times to listen to them."[8] So spoke the angels, and Patrick did as he bade them, and the stories are in the world to this day.

STOPFORD A. BROOKE

COIS NA TEINEADH

(By the Fireside.)

Where glows the Irish hearth with peat
There lives a subtle spell— The faint blue smoke, the gentle heat,
The moorland odours, tell

Of long roads running through a red
Untamed unfurrowed land, With curlews keening overhead,
And streams on either hand;

Black turf-banks crowned with whispering sedge,
And black bog-pools below; While dry stone wall or ragged hedge
Leads on, to meet the glow

From cottage doors, that lure us in
From rainy Western skies, To seek the friendly warmth within,
The simple talk and wise;

Or tales of magic, love and arms
From days when princes met To listen to the lay that charms
The Connacht peasant yet.

There Honour shines through passions dire,
There beauty blends with mirth— Wild hearts, ye never did aspire
Wholly for things of earth!

Cold, cold this thousand years—yet still
On many a time-stained page Your pride, your truth, your dauntless will,
Burn on from age to age.

And still around the fires of peat
Live on the ancient days; There still do living lips repeat
The old and deathless lays.

And when the wavering wreaths ascend,
Blue in the evening air, The soul of Ireland seems to bend
Above her children there.

BARDIC ROMANCES

CHAPTER I

The Story of the Children of Lir

Long ago there dwelt in Ireland the race called by the name of De Danaan, or People of the Goddess Dana. They were a folk who delighted in beauty and gaiety, and in fighting and feasting, and loved to go gloriously apparelled, and to have their weapons and household vessels adorned with jewels and gold. They were also skilled in magic arts, and their harpers could make music so enchanting that a man who heard it would fight, or love, or sleep, or forget all earthly things, as they who touched the strings might will him to do. In later times the Danaans had to dispute the sovranty of Ireland with another race, the Children of Miled, whom men call the Milesians, and after much fighting they were vanquished. Then, by their sorceries and enchantments, when they could not prevail against the invaders, they made themselves invisible, and they have dwelt ever since in the Fairy Mounds and raths of Ireland, where their shining palaces are hidden from mortal eyes. They are now called the Shee, or Fairy Folk of Erinn, and the faint strains of unearthly music that may be heard at times by those who wander at night near to their haunts come from the harpers and pipers who play for the People of Dana at their revels in the bright world underground.

At the time when the tale begins, the People of Dana were still the lords of Ireland, for the Milesians had not yet come. They were divided it is said, into many families and clans; and it seemed good to them that their chiefs should assemble together, and choose one to be king and ruler over the whole people. So they met in a great assembly for this purpose, and found that five of the greatest lords all desired the sovranty of Erin. These five were Bóv the Red, and Ilbrech of Assaroe, and Lir from the Hill of the White Field, which is on Slieve Fuad in Armagh; and Midir the Proud, who dwelt at Slieve Callary in Longford; and Angus of Brugh na Boyna, which is now Newgrange on the river Boyne, where his mighty mound is still to be seen. All the Danaan lords saving these five went into council together, and their decision was to give the sovranty to Bóv the Red, partly because he was the eldest, partly because his father was the Dagda, mightiest of the Danaans, and partly because he was himself the most deserving of the five.

All were content with this, save only Lir, who thought himself the fittest for royal rule; so he went away from the assembly in anger, taking leave of no one. When this became known, the Danaan lords would have pursued Lir, to burn his palace and inflict punishment and wounding on himself for refusing obedience and fealty to him whom the assembly had chosen to reign over them. But Bóv the Red forbade them, for he would not have war among the Danaans; and he said, "I am none the less King of the People of Dana because this man will not do homage to me."

Thus it went on for a long time. But at last a great misfortune befell Lir, for his wife fell ill, and after three nights she died. Sorely did Lir grieve for this, and he fell into a great dejection of spirit, for his wife was very dear to him and was much thought of by all folk, so that her death was counted one of the great events of that time.

Now Bóv the Red came ere long to hear of it, and he said, "If Lir would choose to have my help and friendship now, I can serve him well, for his wife is no longer living, and I have three maidens, daughters of a friend, in fosterage with me, namely, Eva and Aoife[9] and Elva, and there are none fairer and of better name in Erin; one of these he might take to wife." And the lords of the Danaans heard what he said, and answered that it was true and well bethought. So messengers were sent to Lir, to say that if he were willing to yield the sovranty to Bóv the Red, he might make alliance with him and wed one of his foster-

20

children. To Lir, having been thus gently entreated, it seemed good to end the feud, and he agreed to the marriage. So the following day he set out with a train of fifty chariots from the Hill of the White Field and journeyed straight for the palace of Bóv the Red, which was by Lough Derg on the river Shannon.

Arriving there, he found about him nothing but joy and glad faces, for the renewal of amity and concord; and his people were welcomed, and well entreated, and handsomely entertained for the night.

"There sat the three maidens with the Queen"

And there sat the three maidens on the same couch with the Danaan Queen, and Bóv the Red bade Lir choose which one he would have to wife.

"The maidens are all fair and noble," said Lir, "but the eldest is first in consideration and honour, and it is she that I will take, if she be willing."

"The eldest is Eva," said Bóv the Red, "and she will wed thee if it be pleasing to thee." "It is pleasing," said Lir, and the pair were wedded the same night. Lir abode for fourteen days in the palace of Bóv the Red, and then departed with his bride, to make a great wedding-feast among his own people.

In due time after this Eva, wife of Lir, bore him two fair children at a birth, a daughter and a son. The daughter's name was called Fionnuala of the Fair Shoulder, and the son's name was Hugh. And again she bore him two sons, Fiachra and Conn; and at their birth she died. At this Lir was sorely grieved and afflicted, and but for the great love he bore to his four children he would gladly have died too.

When the folk at the palace of Bóv the Red heard that, they also were sorely grieved at the death of their foster-child, and they lamented her with keening and with weeping. Bóv the Red said, "We grieve for this maiden on account of the good man we gave her to, and for his friendship and fellowship; howbeit our friendship shall not be sundered, for we shall give him to wife her sister, namely Aoife."

Word of this was brought to Lir, and he went once more to Lough Derg to the palace of Bóv the Red and there he took to wife Aoife, the fair and wise, and brought her to his own home. And Aoife held the children of Lir and of her sister in honour and affection; for indeed no one could behold these four children without giving them the love of his soul.

For love of them, too, came Bóv the Red often to the house of Lir, and he would take them to his own house at times and let them spend a while there, and then to their own home again. All of the People of Dana who came visiting and feasting to Lir had joy and delight in the children, for their beauty and gentleness; and the love of their father for them was exceeding great, so that he would rise very early every morning to lie down among them and play with them.

Only, alas! a fire of jealousy began to burn at last in the breast of Aoife, and hatred and bitter ill-will grew in her mind towards the children of Lir. And she feigned an illness, and lay under it for the most of a year, meditating a black and evil deed. At last she said that a journey from home might recover her, and she bade her chariot be yoked and set out, taking with her the four children. Fionnuala was sorely unwilling to go with her on that journey, for she had a misgiving, and a prevision of treachery and of kin-slaying against her in the mind of Aoife. Yet she was not able to avoid the mischief that was destined for her.

So Aoife journeyed away from the Hill of the White Field, and when she had come some way she spoke to her people and said, "Kill me, I pray ye, the four children of Lir, who have taken the love of their father from me, and ye may ask of me what reward ye will." "Not so," said they, "by us they shall never be killed; it is an evil deed that you have thought of, and evil it is but to have spoken of it."

When they would not consent to her will, she drew a sword and would have slain the children herself, but her womanhood overcame her and she could not. So they journeyed on westward till they came to the shores of Loch Derryvaragh, and there they made a halt and the horses were outspanned. Aoife bade the children bathe and swim in the lake, and they did so. Then Aoife by Druid spells and witchcraft put upon each of the children the form of a pure white swan, and she cried to them:—

"Out on the lake with you, children of Lir!
Cry with the water-fowl over the mere!
Breed and seed of you ne'er shall I see;
Woeful the tale to your friends shall be."

Then the four swans turned their faces towards the woman, and Fionnuala spoke to her and said, "Evil is thy deed, Aoife, to destroy us thus without a cause, and think not that thou shalt escape punishment for it. Assign us even some period to the ruin and destruction that thou hast brought upon us."

"I shall do that," said Aoife, "and it is this: in your present forms shall ye abide, and none shall release you till the woman of the South be mated with the man of the North. Three hundred years shall ye be upon the waters of Derryvaragh, and three hundred upon the Straits of Moyle between Erinn and Alba,[10] and three hundred in the seas by Erris and Inishglory, and then shall the enchantment have an end."

Upon this, Aoife was smitten with repentance, and she said, "Since I may not henceforth undo what has been done, I give you this, that ye shall keep your human speech, and ye shall sing a sad music such as no music in the world can equal, and ye shall have your reason and your human will, that the bird-shape may not wholly destroy you." Then she became as one possessed, and cried wildly like a prophetess in her trance:—

"Ye with the white faces! Ye with the stammering Gaelic on your tongues!
Soft was your nurture in the King's house—
Now shall ye know the buffeting wind!
Nine hundred years upon the tide.

"The heart of Lir shall bleed!
None of his victories shall stead him now!
Woe to me that I shall hear his groan,
Woe that I have deserved his wrath!"

Then they caught and yoked her horses, and Aoife went on her way till she reached the palace of Bóv the Red. Here she and her folk were welcomed and entertained, and Bóv the Red inquired of her why she had not brought with her the children of Lir.

"I brought them not," she replied, "because Lir loves thee not, and he fears that if he sends his children to thee, thou wouldst capture them and hold them for hostages."

"That is strange," said Bóv the Red, "for I love those children as if they were my own." And his mind misgave him that some treachery had been wrought; and he sent messengers privily northwards to the Hill of the White Field. "For what have ye come?" asked Lir. "Even to bring your children to Bóv the Red," said they. "Did they not reach you with Aoife?" said Lir. "Nay," said the messengers, "but Aoife said you would not permit them to go with her."

Then fear and trouble came upon Lir, for he surmised that Aoife had wrought evil upon the children. So his horses were yoked and he set out upon his road south-westward, until he reached the shores of Loch Derryvaragh. But as he passed by that water, Fionnuala saw the train of horsemen and chariots, and she cried to her brothers to come near to the shore, "for," said she, "these can only be the company of our father who have come to follow and seek for us."

Lir, by the margin of the lake, saw the four swans and heard them talking with human voices, and he halted and spoke to them. Then said Fionnuala: "Know, O Lir, that we are thy four children, and that she who has wrought this ruin upon us is thy wife and our mother's sister, through the bitterness of her jealousy." Lir was glad to know that they were at least living, and he said, "Is it possible to put your own forms upon you again?" "It is not possible," said Fionnuala, "for all the men on earth could not release us until the woman of the South be mated with the man of the North." Then Lir and his people cried aloud in grief and lamentation, and Lir entreated the swans to come on land and abide with him since they had their human reason and speech. But Fionnuala said, "That may not be, for we may not company with men any longer, but abide on the waters of Erinn nine hundred years. But we have still our Gaelic speech, and moreover we have the gift of uttering sad music, so that no man who hears it thinks aught worth in the world save to listen to that music for ever. Do you abide by the shore for this night and we shall sing to you.

So Lir and his people listened all night to the singing of the swans, nor could they move nor speak till morning, for all the high sorrows of the world were in that music, and it plunged them in dreams that could not be uttered.

Next day Lir took leave of his children and went on to the palace of Bóv the Red. Bóv reproached him that he had not brought with him his children. "Woe is me," said Lir, "it was not I that would not bring them; but Aoife there, your own foster-child and their mother's sister, put upon them the forms of four snow-white swans, and there they are on the Loch of Derryvaragh for all men to see; but they have kept still their reason and their human voice and their Gaelic."

Bóv the Red started when he heard this, and he knew that what Lir had said was true. Fiercely he turned to Aoife, and said, "This treachery will be worse, Aoife, for you than for them, for they shall be released in the end of time, but thy punishment shall be for ever." Then he smote her with a druid wand and she became a Demon of the Air, and flew shrieking from the hall, and in that form she abides to this day.

As for Bóv the Red, he came with his nobles and attendants to the shores of Loch Derryvaragh, and there they made an encampment, and the swans conversed with them and sang to them. And as the thing became known, other tribes and clans of the People of Dana would also come from every part of Erinn and stay awhile to listen to the swans and depart again to their homes; and most of all came their own friends and fellow-pupils from the Hill of the White Field. No such music as theirs, say the historians of ancient times, ever was heard in Erinn, for foes who heard it were at peace, and men stricken with pain or sickness felt their ills no more; and the memory of it remained with them when they went away, so that a great peace and sweetness and gentleness was in the land of Erinn for those three hundred years that the swans abode in the waters of Derryvaragh.

But one day Fionnuala said to her brethren, "Do ye know, my dear ones, that the end of our time here is come, all but this night only?" Then great sorrow and distress overcame them, for in the converse with their father and kinsfolk and friends they had half forgotten that they were no longer men, and they loved their home on Loch Derryvaragh, and feared the angry waves of the cold northern sea. But early next day they came to the lough-side to speak with Bóv the Red and with their father, and to bid them farewell, and Fionnuala sang to them her last lament. Then the four swans rose in the air and flew northward till they were seen no more, and great was the grief among those they left behind; and Bóv the Red let it be proclaimed throughout the length and breadth of Erin that no man should henceforth presume to kill a swan, lest it might chance to be one of the children of Lir.

Far different was the dwelling-place which the swans now came to, from that which they had known on Loch Derryvaragh. On either side of them, to north and south, stretched a wide coast far as the eye could see, beset with black rocks and great precipices, and by it ran fiercely the salt, bitter tides of an ever-angry sea, cold, grey, and misty; and their hearts sank to behold it and to think that there they must abide for three hundred years.

Ere long, one night, there came a thick murky tempest upon them, and Fionnuala said, "In this black and violent night, my brothers, we may be driven apart from each other; let us therefore appoint a meeting-place where we may come together again when the tempest is overpast." And they settled to meet at the Seal Rock, for this rock they had now all learned to know.

By midnight the hurricane descended upon the Straits of Moyle, and the waves roared upon the coast with a deafening noise, and thunder bellowed from the sky, and lightning was all the light they had. The swans were driven apart by the violence of the storm, and when at last the wind fell and the seas grew calm once more, Fionnuala found herself alone upon the ocean-tide not far from the Seal Rock. And thus she made her lament:—

"Woe is me to be yet alive!
My wings are frozen to my sides.
Wellnigh has the tempest shattered my heart,
And my comely Hugh parted from me!

"O my beloved ones, my Three,
Who slept under the shelter of my feathers,
Shall you and I ever meet again
Until the dead rise to life?

"Where is Fiachra, where is Hugh?
Where is my fair Conn?
Shall I henceforth bear my part alone?
Woe is me for this disastrous night!"

Fionnuala remained upon the Seal Rock until the morrow morn, watching the tossing waters in all directions around her, until at last she saw Conn coming towards her, and his head drooping and feathers drenched and disarrayed. Joyfully did the sister welcome him; and ere long, behold, Fiachra also approaching them, cold and wet and faint, and the speech was frozen in him that not a word he spake could be understood. So Fionnuala put her wings about him, and said, "If but Hugh came now, how happy should we be!"

In no long time after that they saw Hugh also approaching them across the sea, and his head was dry and his feathers fair and unruffled, for he had found shelter from the gale. Fionnuala put him under her breast, and Conn under her right wing and Fiachra under her left, and covered them wholly with her feathers. "O children," she said to them, "evil though ye think this night to have been, many such a one shall we know from this time forward."

So there the swans continued, suffering cold and misery upon the tides of Moyle; and one while they would be upon the coast of Alba and another upon the coast of Erinn, but the waters they might not leave. At length there came upon them a night of bitter cold and snow such as they had never felt before, and Fionnuala sang this lament:—

"Evil is this life.
The cold of this night,
The thickness of the snow,
The sharpness of the wind—

"How long have they lain together,
Under my soft wings,
The waves beating upon us,
Conn and Hugh and Fiachra?

"Aoife has doomed us,
Us, the four of us,
To-night to this misery—
Evil is this life."

Thus for a long time they suffered, till at length there came upon the Straits of Moyle a night of January so piercing cold that the like of it had never been felt. And the swans were gathered together upon the Seal Rock. The waters froze into ice around them, and each of them became frozen in his place, so that their feet and feathers clung to the rock; and when the day came and they strove to leave the place, the skin of their feet and the feathers of their breasts clove to the rock, they came naked and wounded away.

"Woe is me, O children of Lir," said Fionnuala, "we are now indeed in evil case, for we cannot endure the salt water, yet we may not be away from it; and if the salt water gets into our sores we shall perish of it." And thus she sang:—

"To-night we are full of keening;
No plumage to cover our bodies;
And cold to our tender feet
Are the rough rocks all awash.

"Cruel to us was Aoife,
Who played her magic upon us,
And drove us out to the ocean,
Four wonderful, snow-white swans.

"Our bath is the frothing brine
In the bay by red rocks guarded,
For mead at our father's table
We drink of the salt blue sea.

"Three sons and a single daughter—
In clefts of the cold rocks dwelling,

The hard rocks, cruel to mortals.
—We are full of keening to-night."

So they went forth again upon the Straits of Moyle, and the brine was grievously sharp and bitter to them, but they could not escape it nor shelter themselves from it. Thus they were, till at last their feathers grew again and their sores were healed.

On one day it happened that they came to the mouth of the river Bann in the north of Erinn, and there they perceived a fair host of horsemen riding on white steeds and coming steadily onward from the south-west "Do ye know who yon riders are, children of Lir?" asked Fionnuala. "We know not," said they, "but it is like they are some party of the People of Dana." Then they moved to the margin of the land, and the company they had seen came down to meet them; and behold, it was Hugh and Fergus, the two sons of Bóv the Red, and their nobles and attendants with them, who had long been seeking for the swans along the coast of the Straits of Moyle.

Most lovingly and joyfully did they greet each other and the swans inquired concerning their father Lir, and Bóv the Red, and the rest of their kinsfolk.

"They are well," said the Danaans; "and at this time they are all assembled together in the palace of your father at the Hill of the White Field, where they are holding the Festival of the Age of Youth.[11] They are happy and gay and have no weariness or trouble, save that you are not among them, and that they have not known where you were since you left them at Lough Derryvaragh."

"That is not the tale of our lives," said Fionnuala.

After that the company of the Danaans departed and brought word of the swans to Bóv the Red and to Lir, who were rejoiced to hear that they were living, "for," said they, "the children shall obtain relief in the end of time." And the swans went back to the tides of Moyle and abode there till their time to be in that place had expired.

When that day had come, Fionnuala declared it to them, and they rose up wheeling in the air, and flew westward across Ireland till they came to the Bay of Erris, and there they abode as was ordained. Here it happened that among those of mortal MEN whose dwellings bordered on the bay was a young man of gentle blood, by name Evric, who having heard the singing of the swans came down to speak with them, and became their friend. After that he would often come to hear their music, for it was very sweet to him; and he loved them greatly, and they him. All their story they told him, and he it was who set it down in order, even as it is here narrated.

Much hardship did they suffer from cold and tempest in the waters of the Western Sea, yet not so much as they had to bear by the coasts of the ever-stormy Moyle, and they knew that the day of redemption was now drawing near. In the end of the time Fionnuala said, "Brothers, let us fly to the Hill of the White Field, and see how Lir our father and his household are faring." So they arose and set forward on their airy journey until they reached the Hill of the White Field, and thus it was that they found the place: namely, desolate and thorny before them, with nought but green mounds where once were the palaces and homes of their kin, and forests of nettles growing over them, and never a house nor a hearth. And the four drew closely together and lamented aloud at that sight, for they knew that old times and things had passed away in Erinn, and they were lonely in a land of strangers, where no man lived who could recognise them when they came to their human shapes again. They knew not that Lir and their kin of the People of Dana yet dwelt invisible in the bright world within the Fairy Mounds, for their eyes were holden that they should not see, since other things were destined for them than to join the Danaan folk and be of the company of the immortal Shee.

So they went back again to the Western Sea until the holy Patrick came into Ireland and preached the Faith of the One God and of the Christ. But a man of Patrick's men, namely the Saint Mochaovóg,[12] came to the Island of Inishglory in Erris Bay, and there built himself a little church of stone, and spent his life in preaching to the folk and in prayer. The first night he came to the island the swans heard the sound of his bell ringing at matins on the following morn, and they leaped in terror, and the three brethren left Fionnuala and fled away. Fionnuala cried to them, "What ails you, beloved brothers?" "We know not," said they, "but we have heard a thin and dreadful voice, and we cannot tell what it is." "That is the voice of the bell of Mochaovóg," said Fionnuala, "and it is that bell which shall deliver us and drive away our pains, according to the will of God."

Then the brethren came back and hearkened to the chanting of the cleric until matins were performed. "Let us chant our music now," said Fionnuala. So they began, and chanted a solemn, slow, sweet, fairy song in adoration of the High King of Heaven and of Earth.

Mochaovóg heard that, and wondered, and when he saw the swans he spoke to them and inquired them. They told him they were the children of Lir. "Praised be God for that," said Mochaovóg. "Surely it is for your sakes that I have come to this island above every other island that is in Erinn. Come to land now, and trust in me that your salvation and release are at hand."

So they came to land, and dwelt with Mochaovóg in his own house, and there they kept the canonical hours with him and heard mass. And Mochaovóg caused a good craftsman to make chains of silver for the swans, and put one chain between Fionnuala and Hugh and another between Conn and Fiachra; and they were a joy and solace of mind to the Saint, and their own woe and pain seemed to them dim and far off as a dream.

Now at this time it happened that the King of Connacht was Lairgnen, son of Colman, and he was betrothed to Deoca, daughter of the King of Munster. And so it was that when Deoca came northward to be wedded to Lairgnen she heard the tale of the swans and of their singing, and she prayed the king that he would obtain them for her, for she longed to possess them. But Lairgnen would not ask them of Mochaovóg. Then Deoca set out homeward again, and vowed that she would never return to Lairgnen till she had the swans; and she came as far as the church of Dalua, which is now called Kildaloe, in Clare. Then Lairgnen sent messengers for the birds to Mochaovóg, but he would not give them up.

At this Lairgnen was very wroth, and he went himself to Mochaovóg, and he found the cleric and the four birds at the altar. But Lairgnen seized upon the birds by their silver chains, two in each hand dragged them away to the place where Deoca was; and Mochaovóg followed them. But when they came to Deoca and she had laid her hands upon the birds, behold, their covering of feathers fell off and in their places were three shrunken and feeble old men and one lean and withered old woman, fleshless and bloodless from extreme old age. And Lairgnen was struck with amazement and fear, and went out from that place.

Then Fionnuala said to Mochaovóg, "Come now and baptize us quickly, for our end is near. And if you are grieved at parting from us, know that also to us it is a grief. Do thou make our grave when we are dead, and place Conn at my right side and Fiachra at my left, and Hugh before my face, for thus they were wont to be when I sheltered them on many a winter night by the tides of Moyle."

So Mochaovóg baptized the three brethren and their sister; and shortly afterwards they found peace and death, and they were buried even as Fionnuala had said. And over their tomb a stone was raised, and their names and lineage graved on it in branching Ogham[13]; and lamentation and prayers were made for them, and their souls won to heaven.

But Mochaovóg was sorrowful, and grieved after them so long as he lived on earth.

CHAPTER II

The Quest of the Sons of Turenn

Long ago, when the people of Dana yet held lordship in Erinn, they were sorely afflicted by hordes of sea-rovers named Fomorians who used to harry the country and carry off youths and maidens into captivity. They also imposed cruel and extortionate taxes upon the people, for every kneading trough, and every quern for grinding corn, and every flagstone for baking bread had to pay its tax. And an ounce of gold was paid as a poll-tax for every man, and if any man would not or could not pay, his nose was cut off. Under this tyranny the whole country groaned, but they had none who was able to band them together and to lead them in battle against their oppressors.

Now before this it happened that one of the lords of the Danaans named Kian had married with Ethlinn, daughter of Balor, a princess of the Fomorians. They had a son named Lugh Lamfada, or Lugh of the Long Arm, who grew up into a youth of surpassing beauty and strength. And if his body was noble and mighty, no less so was his mind, for lordship and authority grew to him by the gift of the Immortals, and whatever he purposed that would he perform, whatever it might cost in time or toil, in tears or in blood. Now this Lugh was not brought up in Erinn but in a far-off isle of the western sea, where the sea-god Mananan and the other Immortals nurtured and taught him, and made him fit alike for warfare or for sovranty, when his day should come to work their will on earth. Hither in due time came the report of the grievous and dishonouring oppression wrought by the Fomorians upon the people of Dana, and that report was heard by Lugh. Then Lugh said to his tutors "It were a worthy deed to rescue my father and the people of Erinn from this tyranny; let me go thither and attempt it." And they said to him, "Go, and blessing and victory be with thee." So Lugh armed himself and mounted his fairy steed, and called his friends and foster-brothers about him, and across the bright and heaving surface of the waters they rode like the wind, until they took land in Erinn.

Now the chiefs of the Danaan folk were assembled upon the Hill of Usnach, which is upon the western side of Tara in Meath, in order to meet there the stewards of the Fomorians and to pay them their tribute. As they awaited the arrival of the Fomorians they became aware of a company on horseback, coming from the west, before whom rode a young man who seemed to command them all, and whose countenance was as radiant as the sun upon a dry summer's day, so that the Danaans could scarcely gaze upon it. He rode upon a white horse and was armed with a sword, and on his head was a helmet set with precious stones. The Danaan folk welcomed him as he came among them, and asked him of his name and his business among them. As they were thus talking another band drew near, numbering nine times nine persons, who were the stewards of the Fomorians coming to demand their tribute. They were men of a fierce and swarthy countenance, and as they came haughtily and arrogantly forward, the Danaans all rose up to do them honour. Then Lugh said:

"Why do ye rise up before that grim and ill-looking band and not before us?"

Said the King of Erinn, "We needs must do so, for if they saw but a child of a month old sitting down when they came near they would hold it cause enough to attack and slay us."

"I am greatly minded to slay them," said Lugh; and he repeated it, "very greatly minded."

"That would be bad for us," said the King, "for our death and destruction would surely follow."

"Ye are too long under oppression," said Lugh, and gave the word for onset. So he and his comrades rushed upon the Fomorians, and in a moment the hillside rang with blows and with the shouting of warriors. In no long time all of the Fomorians were slain save nine men, and these were taken alive and brought before Lugh.

"Ye also should be slain," said Lugh, "but that I am minded to send you as ambassadors to your King. Tell him that he may seek homage and tribute where he will henceforth, but Ireland will pay him none for ever."

Then the Fomorians went northwards away, and the people of Dana made them ready for war, and made Lugh their captain and war-lord, for the sight of his face heartened them, and made them strong, and they marvelled that they had endured their slavery so long.

In the meantime word was brought to Balor of the Mighty Blows, King of the Fomorians, and to his queen Kethlinn of the Twisted Teeth, of the shame and destruction that had been done to their stewards, and they assembled a great host of the sea-rovers and manned their war-ships, and the Northern Sea was white with the foam of their oarblades as they swept down upon the shores of Erinn. And Balor commanded them, saying, "When ye have utterly destroyed and subdued the people of Dana, then make fast your ships with cables to the land of Erinn, and tow it here to the north of us into the region of ice and snow, and it shall trouble us no longer." So the host of Balor took land by the Falls of Dara[14] and began plundering and devastating the province of Connacht.

Then Lugh sent messengers abroad to bring his host together, and among them was his own father, Kian, son of Canta. And as Kian went northwards on his errand to rouse the Ulster men, and was now come to the plain of Murthemny near by Dundealga,[15] he saw three warriors armed and riding across the plain. Now these three were the sons of Turenn, by name Brian and Iuchar and Iucharba. And there was an ancient blood-feud between the house of Canta and the house of Turenn, so that they never met without bloodshed.

Then Kian thought to himself, "If my brothers Cu and Kethan were here there might be a pretty fight, but as they are three to one I would do better to fly." Now there was a herd of wild swine near by; and Kian changed himself by druidic sorceries into a wild pig and fell to rooting up the earth along with the others.

When the sons of Turenn came up to the herd, Brian said, "Brothers, did ye see the warrior wh' just now was journeying across the plain?"

"We saw him," said they.

"What is become of him?" said Brian.

"Truly, we cannot tell," said the brothers.

"It is good watch ye keep in time of war!" said Brian; "but I know what has taken him out of our sight, for he struck himself with a magic wand, and changed himself into the form of one of yonder swine, and he is rooting the earth among them now. Wherefore," said Brian, "I deem that he is no friend to us."

"If so, we have no help for it," said they, "for the herd belongs to some man of the Danaans; and even if we set to and begin to kill the swine, the pig of druidism might be the very one to escape."

"Have ye learned so little in your place of studies," said Brian, "that ye cannot distinguish a druidic beast from a natural beast?" And with that he smote his two brothers with a magic wand, and changed them into two slender, fleet hounds, and they darted in among the herd. Then all the herd scattered and fled, but the hounds separated the druidic pig and chased it towards a wood where Brian awaited it. As it passed, Brian flung his spear, and it pierced the chest of the pig and brought it down. The pig screamed, "Evil have you done to cast at me."

Brian said, "That hath the sound of human speech!"

"I am in truth a man," said the pig, "and I am Kian, son of Canta, and I pray you show me mercy."

"That will we," said Iuchar and Iucharba, "and sorry are we for what has happened."

"Nay," said Brian, "but I swear by the Wind and the Sun that if thou hadst seven lives I would take them all."

"Grant me a favour then," said Kian.

"We shall grant it," said Brian.

"Let me," said Kian, "return into my own form that I may die in the shape of a man."

"I had liefer kill a man than a pig," said Brian. Then Kian became a man again and stood before them, the blood trickling from his breast.

"I have outwitted you now," cried he, "for if ye had killed a pig ye would have paid a pig's eric,[16] but now ye shall pay the eric of a man. Never was greater eric in the land of Erinn than that which ye shall pay; and I swear that the very weapons with which ye slay me shall tell the tale to the avenger of blood."

"Then you shall be slain with no weapons at all," said Brian; and they picked up the stones on the Plain of Murthemny and rained them upon him till he was all one wound, and he died. So they buried him as deep as the height of a man, and went their way to join the host of Lugh.

When the host was assembled, Lugh led them into Connacht and smote the Fomorians and drove them to their ships, but of this the tale tells not here. But when the fight was done, Lugh asked of his comrades if they had seen his father in the fight and how it fared with him. They said they had not seen him. Then Lugh made search among the dead, and they found not Kian there. "Were Kian alive he would be here," said Lugh, "and I swear by the Wind and the Sun that I will not eat or drink till I know what has befallen him."

On their return the Danaan host passed by the Plain of Murthemny, and when they came near the place of the murder the stones cried aloud to Lugh. And Lugh listened, and they told him of the deed of the sons of

Turenn. Then Lugh searched for the place of a new grave, and when he had found it he caused it to be dug, and the body of his father was raised up, and Lugh saw that it was but a litter of wounds. And he cried out: "O wicked and horrible deed!" and he kissed his father and said, "I am sick from this sight, my eyes are blind from it, my ears are deaf from it, my heart stands still from it. Ye gods that I adore, why was I not here when this crime was done? a man of the children of Dana slain by his fellows." And he lamented long and bitterly. Then Kian was again laid in his grave, and a mound was heaped over it and a pillar-stone set thereon and his name written in Ogham, and a dirge was sung for him.

After that Lugh departed to Tara, to the Court of the High King, and he charged his people to say nothing of what had happened until he himself had made it known.

When he reached Tara with his victorious host the King placed Lugh at his own right hand before all the princes and lords of the Danaan folk. Lugh looked round about him, and saw the sons of Turenn sitting among the assembly; and they were among the best and strongest and the handsomest of those who were present at that time; nor had any borne themselves better in the fight with the sea-rovers. Then Lugh asked of the King that the chain of silence might be shaken; and the assembly heard it, and gave their attention to Lugh. And Lugh said:

"O King, and ye princes of the People of Dana, I ask what vengeance would each of you exact upon a man who had foully murdered your father?"

Then they were all astonished, and the King answered and said:

"Surely it is not the father of Lugh Lamfada who has thus been slain?"

"Thou hast said it," said Lugh, "and those who did the deed are listening to me now, and know it better than I."

The King said, "Not in one day would I slay the murderer of my father, but I would tear from him a limb day by day till he were dead."

And so spake all the lords of the Danaans, and the Sons of Turenn among the rest.

"They have sentenced themselves, the murderers of my father," said Lugh. "Nevertheless I shall accept an eric from them, and if they will pay it, it shall be well; but if not, I shall not break the peace of the King's Assembly and of his sanctuary, but let them beware how they leave the Hall Tara until they have made me satisfaction."

"Had I slain your father," said the High King, "glad should I be to have an eric accepted for his blood."

Then the Sons of Turenn whispered among themselves. "It is to us that Lugh is speaking," said Iuchar and Iucharba, "let us confess and have the eric assessed upon us, for he has got knowledge of our deed."

"Nay," said Brian, "but he may be seeking for an open confession, and then perchance he would not accept an eric."

But the two brethren said to Brian, "Do thou confess because thou art the eldest, or if thou do not, then we shall."

So Brian, son of Turenn, rose up and said to Lugh: "It is to us thou hast spoken, Lugh, since thou knowest there is enmity of old time between our houses; and if thou wilt have it that we have slain thy father, then declare our eric and we shall pay it."

"I will take an eric from you," said Lugh, "and if it seem too great, I will remit a portion of it."

"Declare it, then," said the Sons of Turenn.

"This it is," said Lugh.

"Three apples.

"The skin of a pig.

"A spear.

"Two steeds and a chariot.

"Seven swine.

"A whelp of a dog.

"A cooking spit.

"Three shouts on a hill."

"We would not consider heavy hundreds or thousands of these things," said the Sons of Turenn, "but we misdoubt thou hast some secret purpose against us."

"I deem it no small eric," said Lugh, "and I call to witness the High King and lords of the Danaans that I shall ask no more; and do ye on your side give me guarantees for the fulfilment of it."

So the High King and the lords of the Danaans entered into bonds with Lugh and with the Sons of Turenn that the eric should be paid and should wipe out the blood of Kian.

"Now," said Lugh, "it is better forme to give you fuller knowledge of the eric. The three apples that I have demanded of you are the apples that grow in the garden of the Hesperides, in the east of the world, and none but these will do. Thus it is with them: they are the colour of bright gold, and as large as the head of a month-old child; the taste of them is like honey; if he who eats them has any running sore or evil disease it is healed by them; they may be eaten and eaten and never be less. I doubt, O young heroes, if ye will get these apples, for those who guard them know well an ancient prophecy that one day three knights from the western world would come to attempt them.

"As for the skin of the pig, that is a treasure of Tuish, the King of Greece. If it be laid upon a wounded man it will make him whole and well, if only it overtake the breath of life in him. And do ye know what is the spear that I demanded?"

"We do not," said they.

"It is the poisoned spear of Peisear, the King of Persia, and so fierce is the spirit of war in it that it must be kept in a pot of soporific herbs or it would fly out raging for death. And do ye know what are the two horses and the chariot ye must get?"

"We do not know," said they.

"The steeds and the chariot belong to Dobar, King of Sicily. They are magic steeds and can go indifferently over land and sea, nor can they be killed by any weapon unless they be torn in pieces and their bones cannot be found. And the seven pigs are the swine of Asal, King of the Golden Pillars, which may be slain and eaten every night and the next morning they are alive again.

"And the hound-whelp I asked of you is the whelp of the King of Iorroway, that can catch and slay any beast in the world; hard it is to get possession of that whelp.

"The cooking spit is one of the spits that the fairy women of the Island of Finchory have in their kitchen.

"And the hill on which ye must give three shouts is the hill where dwells Mochaen in the north of Lochlann. Now Mochaen and his sons have it as a sacred ordinance that they permit not any man to raise a shout upon their hill. With him it was that my father was trained to arms, and if I forgave ye his death, yet would Mochaen not forgive it.

"And now ye know the eric which ye have to pay for the slaying of Kian, son of Canta."

Astonishment and despair overcame the Sons of Turenn when they learned the meaning of the eric of Lugh, and they went home to tell the tidings to their father.

"This is an evil tale," said Turenn; "I doubt but death and doom shall come from your seeking of that eric, and it is but right they should. Yet it may be that ye shall obtain the eric if Lugh or Mananan will help you to it. Go now to Lugh, and ask him for the loan of the fairy steed of Mananan, which was given him to ride over the sea into Erinn. He will refuse you, for he will say that the steed is but lent to him and he may not make a loan of a loan. Then ask him for the loan of Ocean Sweeper, which is the magic boat of Mananan, and that he must give, for it is a sacred ordinance with Lugh not to refuse a second petition."

So they went to Lugh, and it all fell out as Turenn had told them, and they went back to Turenn.

"Ye have done something towards the eric," said Turenn, "but not much. Yet Lugh would be well pleased that ye brought him whatever might serve him when the Fomorians come to the battle again, and well pleased would he be that ye might get your death in bringing it. Go now, my sons, and blessing and victory be with you."

Then the Sons of Turenn went down to the harbour on the Boyne river where the Boat of Mananan was, and Ethne their sister with them. And when they reached the place, Ethne broke into lamentations and weeping; but Brian said, "Weep not, dear sister, but let us go forth gaily to great deeds. Better a hundred deaths in the quest of honour than to live and die as cowards and sluggards." But Ethne said, "ye are banished from Erinn—never was there a sadder deed." Then they put forth from the river-mouth of the Boyne and soon the fair coasts of Erinn faded out of sight. "And now," said they among themselves, "what course shall we steer?"

"'Bear us swiftly, Boat of Mananan, to the Garden of the Hesperides'"

"No need to steer the Boat of Mananan," said Brian; and he whispered to the Boat, "Bear us swiftly, Boat of Mananan, to the Garden of the Hesperides"; and the spirit of the Boat heard him and it leaped eagerly forward, lifting and dipping over the rollers and throwing up an arch of spray each side of its bows wherein sat a rainbow when the sun shone upon it; and so in no long time they drew nigh to the coast where was the far-famed garden of the Golden Apples.

"And now, how shall we set about the capture of the apples?" said Brian.

"Draw sword and fight for them," said Iuchar and Iucharba, "and if we are the stronger, we shall win them, and if not, we shall fall, as fall we surely must ere the eric for Kian be paid."

"Nay," said Brian, "but whether we live or die, let not men say of us that we went blind and headlong to our tasks, but rather that we made the head help the hand, and that we deserved to win even though we lost. Now my counsel is that we approach the garden in the shape of three hawks, strong of wing, and that we hover about until the Wardens of the Tree have spent all their darts and javelins in casting at us, and then let us swoop down suddenly and bear off each of us an apple if we may."

So it was agreed; and Brian struck himself and each of the brothers with a druid wand, and they became three beautiful, fierce, and strong-winged hawks. When the Wardens perceived them, they shouted and threw showers of arrows and darts at them, but the hawks evaded all of these until the missiles were spent, and then seized each an apple in his talons. But Brian seized two, for he took one in his beak as well. Then they flew as swiftly as they might to the shore where they had left their boat. Now the King of that garden had three fair daughters, to whom the apples and the garden were very dear, and he transformed the maidens into three griffins, who pursued the hawks. And the griffins threw darts of fire, as it were lightning, at the hawks.

"Brian!" then cried Iuchar and his brother, "we are being burnt by these darts—we are lost unless we can escape them."

On this, Brian changed himself and his brethren into three swans, and they plunged into the sea, and the burning darts were quenched. Then the griffins gave over the chase, and the Sons of Turenn made for their boat, and they embarked with the four apples. Thus their first quest was ended.

After that they resolved to seek the pigskin from the King of Greece, and they debated how they should come before him. "Let us," said Brian, "assume the character and garb of poets and men of learning, for such are wont to come from Ireland and to travel foreign lands, and in that character shall the Greeks receive us best, for such men have honour among them." "It is well said," replied the brothers, "yet we have no poems in our heads, and how to compose one we know not."

Howbeit they dressed their hair in the fashion of the poets of Erinn, and went up to the palace of Tuish the King. The doorkeeper asked of them who they were, and what was their business.

"We are bards from Ireland," they said, "and we have come with a poem to the King."

"Let them be admitted," said the King, when the doorkeeper brought him that tale; "they have doubtless come thus far to seek a powerful patron."

So Brian and Iuchar and Iucharba came in and were made welcome, and were entertained, and then the minstrels of the King of Greece chanted the lays of that country before them. After that came the turn of the stranger bards, and Brian asked his brethren if they had anything to recite.

"We have not," said they; "we know but one art—to take what we want by the strong hand if we may, and if we may not, to die fighting."

"That is a difficult art too," said Brian; "let us see how we thrive with the poetry."

So he rose up and recited this lay:—

"Mighty is thy fame, O King,
Towering like a giant oak;
For my song I ask no thing
Save a pigskin for a cloak.

"When a neighbour with his friend
Quarrels, they are ear to ear;
Who on us their store shall spend
Shall be richer than they were.

"Armies of the storming wind—
Raging seas, the sword's fell stroke—
Thou hast nothing to my mind
Save thy pigskin for a cloak."

"That is a very good poem," said the King, "but one word of its meaning I do not understand."

"I will interpret it for you," said Brian:—

"Mighty is thy fame, O King,
Towering like a giant oak."

"That is to say, as the oak surpasses all the other trees of the forest, so do you surpass all the kings of the world in goodness, in nobleness, and in liberality.

"A pigskin for a cloak."

"That is the skin of the pig of Tuish which I would fain receive as the reward for my lay."

"When a neighbour with his friend
Quarrels, they are ear to ear."

"That is to signify that you and I shall be about each other's ears over the skin, unless you are willing to give it to me. Such is the sense of my poem," said Brian, son of Turenn.

"I would praise your poem more," said the King, "if there were not so much about my pigskin in it. Little sense have you, O man of poetry, to make that request of me, for not to all the poets, scholars, and lords of the world would I give that skin of my own free will. But what I will do is this—I will give the full of that skin of red gold thrice over in reward for your poem."

"Thanks be to you," said Brian, "for that. I knew that I asked too much, but I knew also thou wouldst redeem the skin amply and generously. And now let the gold be duly measured out in it, for greedy am I, and I will not abate an ounce of it."

The servants of the King were then sent with Brian and his brothers to the King's treasure-chamber to measure out the gold. As they did so, Brian suddenly snatched the skin from the hands of him who held it, and swiftly wrapped it round his body. Then the three brothers drew sword and made for the door, and a great fight arose in the King's palace. But they hewed and thrust manfully on every side of them, and though sorely wounded they fought their way through and escaped to the shore, and drove their boat out to sea, when the skin of the magic pig quickly made them whole and sound again. And thus the second quest of the Sons of Turenn had its end.

"Let us now," said Brian, "go to seek the spear of the King of Persia."

"In what manner of guise shall we go before the King of Persia?" said his brothers.

"As we did before the King of Greece," said Brian.

"That guise served us well with the King of Greece," replied they; "nevertheless, O Brian, this business of professing to be poets, when we are but swordsmen, is painful to us."

However, they dressed their hair in the manner of poets and went up boldly to the palace of King Peisear of Persia, saying, as before, that they were wandering bards from Ireland who had a poem to recite before the King; and as they passed through the courtyard they marked the spear drowsing in its pot of sleepy herbs. They were made welcome, and after listening to the lays of the King's minstrel, Brian rose and sang:—

"'Tis little Peisear cares for spears,
Since armies, when his face they see,
All overcome with panic fears
Without a wound they turn and flee.

"The Yew is monarch of the wood,
No other tree disputes its claim.
The shining shaft in venom stewed
Flies fiercely forth to kill and maim."

"'Tis a very good poem," said the King, "but, O bard from Erinn, I do not understand your reference to my spear."

"It is merely this," replied Brian, "that I would like your spear as a reward for my poem."

Then the King stared at Brian, and his beard bristled with anger, and he said, "Never was a greater reward paid for any poem than not to adjudge you guilty of instant death for your request."

Then Brian flung at the king the fourth golden apple which he had taken from the Garden of the Hesperides, and it dashed out his brains. Immediately the brothers all drew sword and made for the courtyard. Here they seized the magic spear, and with it and with their swords they fought their way clear, not without many wounds, and escaped to their boat. And thus ended the third quest of the Sons of Turenn.

Now having come safely and victoriously through so many straits and perils, they began to be merry and hoped that all the eric might yet be paid. So they sailed away with high hearts to the Island of Sicily, to get the two horses and the chariot of the King, and the Boat of Mananan bore them swiftly and well.

Having arrived here, they debated among themselves as to how they should proceed; and they agreed to present themselves as Irish mercenary soldiers—for such were wont in those days to take service with foreign kings—until they should learn where the horses and the chariot were kept, and how they should come at them. Then they went forward, and found the King and his lords in the palace garden taking the air.

The Sons of Turenn then paid homage to him, and he asked them of their business.

"We are Irish mercenary soldiers," they said, "seeking our wages from the kings of the world." "Are ye willing to take service with me?" said the King. "We are," said they, "and to that end are we come."

Then their contract of military service was made, and they remained at the King's court for a month and a fortnight, and did not in all that time come to see the steeds or the chariot. At last Brian said,

"Things are going ill with us, my brethren, in that we know no more at this day of the steeds or of the chariot than when we first arrived at this place."

"What shall we do, then?" said they.

"Let us do this," said Brian. "Let us gird on our arms and all our marching array, and tell the King that we shall quit his service unless he show us the chariot.

And so they did; and the King said, "To-morrow shall be a gathering and parade of all my host, and the chariot shall be there, and ye shall see it if ye have a mind."

So the next day the steeds were yoked and the chariot was driven round a great plain before the King and his lords. Now these steeds could run as well on sea as on dry land, and they were swifter than the winds of March. As the chariot came round the second time, Brian and his brothers seized the horses' heads, and Brian took the charioteer by the foot and flung him out over the rail, and they all leaped into the chariot and drove away. Such was the swiftness of their driving that they were out of sight ere the King and his men knew rightly what had befallen. And thus ended the fourth quest of the Sons of Turenn.

Next they betook themselves to the court of Asal, King of the Golden Pillars, to get the seven swine which might be eaten every night and they would be whole and well on the morrow morn.

But it had now been noised about every country that three young heroes from Erinn were plundering the kings of the world of their treasures in payment of a mighty eric; and when they arrived at the Land of the Golden Pillars they found the harbour guarded and a strait watch kept, that no one who might resemble the Sons of Turenn should enter.

But Asal the King came to the harbour-mouth and spoke with the heroes, for he was desirous to see those who had done the great deeds that he had heard of. He asked them if it were true that they had done such things, and why. Then Brian told him the story of the mighty eric which had been laid upon them, and what they had done and suffered in fulfilling it. "Why," said King Asal, "have ye now come to my country?"

"For the seven swine," said Brian, "to take them with us as a part of that eric."

"How do you mean to get them?" asked the King.

"With your goodwill," replied Brian, "if so it may be, and to pay you therefore with all the wealth we now have, which is thanks and love, and to stand by your side hereafter in any strait or quarrel you may enter into. But if you will not grant us the swine, and we may not be quit of our eric without them, we shall even take them as we may, and as we have beforetime taken mighty treasures from mighty kings."

Then King Asal went into counsel with his lords, and he advised that the swine be given to the Sons of Turenn, partly for that he was moved with their desperate plight and the hardihood they had shown, and partly that they might get them whether or no. To this they all agreed, and the Sons of Turenn were invited to come ashore, where they were courteously and hospitably entertained in the King's palace. On the morrow the pigs were given to them, and great was their gladness, for never before had they won a treasure without toil and blood. And they vowed that, if they should live, the name of Asal should be made by them a great and shining name, for his compassion and generosity which he had shown them. This, then, was the fifth quest of the Sons of Turenn.

"And whither do ye voyage now?" said Asal to them.

"We go," said they, "to Iorroway for the hound's whelp which is there."

"Take me with you, then," said Asal, "for the King of Iorroway is husband to my daughter, and I may prevail upon him to grant you the hound without combat."

So the King's ship was manned and provisioned, and the Sons of Turenn laid up their treasures in the Boat of Mananan, and they all sailed joyfully forth to the pleasant kingdom of Iorroway. But here, too, they found all the coasts and harbours guarded, and entrance was forbidden them. Then Asal declared who he was, and him they allowed to land, and he journeyed to where his son-in-law, the King of Iorroway, was. To him Asal related the whole story of the sons of Turenn, and why they were come to that kingdom.

"Thou wert a fool," said the King of Iorroway, "to have come on such a mission. There are no three heroes in the world to whom the Immortals have granted such grace that they should get my hound either by favour or by fight."

"That is not a good word," said Asal, "for the treasures they now possess have made them yet stronger than they were, and these they won in the teeth of kings as strong as thou." And much more he said to him to persuade him to yield up the hound, but in vain. So Asal took his way back to the haven where the Sons of Turenn lay, and told them his tidings.

Then the Sons of Turenn seized the magic spear, and the pigskin, and with a rush like that of three eagles descending from a high cliff upon a lamb-fold they burst upon the guards of the King of Iorroway. Fierce and fell was the combat that ensued, and many times the brothers were driven apart, and all but overborne by the throng of their foes. But at last Brian perceived where the King of Iorroway was directing the fight, and he cut his way to him, and having smitten him to the ground, he bound him and carried him out of the press to the haven-side where Asal was.

"There," he said, "is your son-in-law for you Asal, and I swear by my sword that I had more easily killed him thrice than once to bring him thus bound to you."

"That is very like," said Asal; "but now hold him to ransom."

So the people of Iorroway gave the hound to the Sons of Turenn as a ransom for their King, and the King was released, and friendship and alliance were made between them. And with joyful hearts the Sons of Turenn bade farewell to the King of Iorroway and to Asal, and departed on their way. Thus was the sixth of their quests fulfilled.

Now Lugh Lamfada desired to know how the Sons of Turenn had fared, and whether they had got any portion of the great eric that might be serviceable to him when the Fomorians should return for one more struggle. And by sorcery and divination it was revealed to him how they had thriven, and that nought remained to be won save the cooking-spit of the sea-nymphs, and to give the three shouts upon the hill. Lugh then by druidic art caused a spell of oblivion and forgetfulness to descend upon the Sons of Turenn, and put into their hearts withal a yearning and passion to return to their native land of Erinn. They forgot, therefore, that a portion of the eric was still to win, and they bade the Boat of Mananan bear them home with their treasures, for they deemed that they should now quit them of all their debt for the blood of Kian and live free in their father's home, having done such things and won such fame as no three brothers had ever done since the world began.

At the Brugh of Boyne, where they had started on their quest, their boat came ashore again, and as they landed they wept for joy, and falling on their knees they kissed the green sod of Erinn. Then they took up their treasures and journeyed to Ben Edar,[17] where the High King of Ireland, and Lugh with him, were holding an Assembly of the People of Dana. But when Lugh heard that they were on their way he put on his cloak of invisibility and withdrew privily to Tara.

When the brethren arrived at Ben Edar, the High King of the lords of the Danaans gave them welcome and applause, for all were rejoiced that the stain of ancient feud and bloodshed should be wiped out, and that the Children of Dana should be at peace within their borders. Then they sought for Lugh to deliver over the eric, but he was not to be found. And Brian said, "He has gone to Tara to avoid us, having heard that we were coming with our treasures and weapons of war."

Word was then sent to Lugh at Tara that the Sons of Turenn were at Ben Edar, and the eric with them.

"Let them pay it over to the High King," said Lugh.

So it was done; and when Lugh had tidings that the High King had the eric, he returned to Ben Edar.

Then the eric was laid before him, and Brian said, "Is the debt paid, O Lugh, son of Kian?"

Lugh said, "Truly there is here the price of any man's death; but it is not lawful to give a quittance for an eric that is not complete. Where is the cooking-spit from the Island of Finchory? and have ye given the three shouts upon the Hill of Mochaen?"

At this word Brian and Iuchar and Iucharba fell prone upon the ground, and were speechless awhile from grief and dismay. After a while they left the Assembly like broken men, with hanging heads and with heavy steps, and betook themselves to Dún Turenn, where they found their father, and they told him all that had befallen them since they had parted with him and set forth on the Quest. Thus they passed the night in gloom and evil forebodings, and on the morrow they went down once more to the place where the Boat of Mananan was moored. And Ethne their sister accompanied them, wailing and lamenting, but no words of cheer had they now to say to her, for now they began to comprehend that a mightier and a craftier mind had caught them in the net of fate. And whereas they had deemed themselves heroes and victors in the most glorious quest whereof the earth had record, they now knew that they were but as arrows in the hands of a laughing archer, who shoots one at a stag and one at the heart of a foe, and one, it may be, in sheer wantonness, and to try his bow, over a cliff edge into the sea.

However, they put forth in their magic boat, but in no wise could they direct it to the Isle of Finchory, and a quarter of a year they traversed the seaways and never could get tidings of that island. At last Brian fashioned for himself by magic art a water-dress, with a helmet of crystal, and into the depths of the sea he plunged. Here, the story tells, he searched hither and thither for a fortnight, till at last he found that island, which was an island indeed with the sea over it and around it and beneath it. There dwelt the red-haired ocean-nymphs in glittering palaces among the sea-flowers, and they wrought fair embroidery with gold and jewels, and sang, as they wrought, a fairy music like the chiming of silver bells. Three fifties of them sat or played in their great hall as Brian entered, and they gazed on him but spoke no word. Then Brian strode to the wide hearth, and without a word he seized from it a spit that was made of beaten gold, and turned again to go. But at that the laughter of the sea-maidens rippled through the hall and one of them said:

"Thou art a bold man, Brian, and bolder than thou knowest; for if thytwo brothers were here, the weakest of us could vanquish all the three. Nevertheless, take the spit for thy daring; we had never granted it for thy prayers."

So Brian thanked them and bade farewell, and he rose to the surface of the water. Ere long his brethren perceived him as he shouldered the waves on the bosom of the deep, and they sailed to where he was and took him on board. And thus ended the quest for the seventh portion of the eric of Kian.

After that their hopes revived a little, and they set sail for the land of Lochlann, in which was the Hill of Mochaen. When they had arrived at the hill Mochaen came out to meet them with his three sons, Corc and Conn and Hugh; nor did the Sons of Turenn ever behold a band of grimmer and mightier warriors than those four.

"What seek ye here?" asked Mochaen of them They told him that it had been laid upon them to give three shouts upon the hill.

"It hath been laid upon me," said Mochaen, "to prevent this thing."

Then Brian and Mochaen drew sword and fell furiously upon each other, and their fighting was like that of two hungry lions or two wild bulls, until at last Brian drove his sword into the throat of Mochaen, and he died.

With that the Sons of Mochaen and the Sons of Turenn rushed fiercely upon each other. Long and sore was the strife that they had, and the blood that fell made red the grassy place wherein they fought. Not one of them but received wounds that pierced him through and through, and that heroes of less hardihood had died of a score of times. But in the end the sons of Mochaen fell, and Brian, Iuchar, and Iucharba lay over them in a swoon like death.

After a while Brian's senses came back to him, and he said, "Do ye live, dear brothers, or how is it with you?" "We are as good as dead," said they; "let us be."

"Arise," then said Brian, "for truly I feel death coming swiftly upon us, and we have yet to give the three shouts upon the hill."

"We cannot stir," said Iuchar and Iucharba. Then Brian rose to his knees and to his feet, and he lifted up his two brothers while the blood of all three streamed down to their feet, and they raised their voices as best they might, and gave three hoarse cries upon the Hill of Mochaen. And thus was the last of the epic fulfilled.

Then they bound up their wounds, and Brian placed himself between the two brothers, and slowly and painfully they made their way to the boat, and put out to sea for Ireland. And as they lay in the stupor of faintness in the boat, one murmured to himself, "I see the Cape of Ben Edar and the coast of Turenn, and Tara of the Kings." Then Iuchar and Iucharba entreated Brian to lift their heads upon his breast. "Let us but see the land of Erinn again," said they, "the hills around Tailtin, and the dewy plain of Bregia, and the quiet waters of the Boyne and our father's Dún thereby, and healing will come to us; or if death come we can endure it after that." Then Brian raised them up; and they saw that they were now near by under Ben Edar; and at the Strand of the Bull[18] they took land. They were then conveyed to the Dún of Turenn, and life was still in them when they were laid in their father's hall.

And Brian said to Turenn, "Go now, dear father, with all speed to Lugh at Tara. Give him the cooking-spit, and tell how thou hast found us after giving our three shouts upon the Hill of Mochaen. Then beseech him that he yield thee the loan of the pigskin of the King of Greece, for if it be laid upon us while the life is yet in us, we shall recover. We have won the eric, and it may be that he will not pursue us to our death."

Turenn went to Lugh and gave him the spit of the sea-nymphs, and besought him for the lives of his sons.

Lugh was silent for a while, but his countenance did not change, and he said, "Thou, old man, seest nought but the cloud of sorrow wherein thou art encompassed. But I hear from above it the singing of the Immortal Ones, who tell to one another the story of this land. Thy sons must die; yet have I shown to them more mercy than they showed to Kian. I have forgiven them; nor shall they live to slay their own immortality, but the royal bards of Erinn and the old men in the chimney corners shall tell of their glory and their fate as long as the land shall endure."

Then Turenn bowed his white head and went sorrowfully back to Dún Turenn; and he told his sons of the words that Lugh had said. And with that the sons of Turenn kissed each other, and the breath of life departed from them, and they died. And Turenn died also, for his heart was broken in him; and Ethne his daughter buried them in one grave. Thus, then, ends the tale of the Quest of the Eric and the Fate of the Sons of Turenn.

41

CHAPTER III

The Secret of Labra

In very ancient days there was a King in Ireland named Labra, who was called Labra the Sailor for a certain voyage that he made. Now Labra was never seen save by one man, once a year, without a hood that covered his head and ears. But once a year it was his habit to let his hair be cropped, and the person to do this was chosen by lot, for the King was accustomed to put to death instantly the man who had cropped him. And so it happened that on a certain year the lot fell on a young man who was the only son of a poor widow, who dwelt near by the palace of the King. When she heard that her son had been chosen she fell on her knees before the King and besought him, with tears, that her son, who was her only support and all she had in the world, might not suffer death as was customary. The King was moved by her grief and her entreaties, and at last he consented that the young man should not be slain provided that he vowed to keep secret to the day of his death what he should see. The youth agreed to this and he vowed by the Sun and the Wind that he would never, so long as he lived, reveal to man what he should learn when he cropped the King's hair.

So he did what was appointed for him and went home. But when he did so he had no peace for the wonder of the secret that he had learned preyed upon his mind so that he could not rest for thinking of it and longing to reveal it, and at last he fell into a wasting sickness from it, and was near to die. Then there was brought to see him a wise druid, who was skilled in all maladies of the mind and body, and after he had talked with the youth he said to his mother, "Thy son is dying of the burden of a secret which he may not reveal to any man, but until he reveals it he will have no ease. Let him, therefore, walk along the high way till he comes to a place where four roads meet. Let him then turn to the right, and the first tree that he shall meet on the roadside let him tell the secret to it, and so it may be he shall be relieved, and his vow will not be broken."

The mother told her son of the druid's advice, and next day he went upon his way till he came to four cross roads, and he took the road upon the right, and the first tree he found was a great willow-tree. So the young man laid his cheek against the bark, and he whispered the secret to the tree, and as he turned back homeward he felt lightened of his burden, and he leaped and sang, and ere many days were past he was as well and light hearted as ever he had been in his life.

Some while after that it happened that the King's harper, namely Craftiny, broke the straining-post of his harp and went out to seek for a piece of wood wherewith to mend it. And the first timber he found that would fit the purpose was the willow-tree by the cross roads. He cut it down, therefore, and took as much as would give him a new straining-post, and he bore it home with him and mended his harp with it. That night he played after meat before the King and his lords as he was wont, but whatever he played and sang the folk that listened to him seemed to hear only one thing, "Two horse's ears hath Labra the Sailor."

Then the King plucked off his hood, and after that he made no secret of his ears and none suffered on account of them thenceforward.

CHAPTER IV

King Iubdan and King Fergus

It happened on a day when Fergus son of Leda was King of Ulster, that Iubdan, King of the Leprecauns or Wee Folk, of the land of Faylinn, held a great banquet and assembly of the lords and princes of the Wee Folk. And all their captains and men of war came thither, to show their feats before the King, among whom was the strong man, namely Glowar, whose might was such that with his battle-axe he could hew down a thistle at one stroke. Thither also came the King's heir-apparent, Tiny, son of Tot, and the Queen Bebo with her maidens; and there were also the King's harpers and singing-men, and the chief poet of the court, who was called Eisirt.

All these sat down to the feast in due order and precedence, with Bebo on the King's right hand and the poet on his left, and Glowar kept the door. Soon the wine began to flow from the vats of dark-red yew-wood, and the carvers carved busily at great haunches of roast hares and ribs of field-mice; and they all ate and drank, and loudly the hall rang with gay talk and laughter, and the drinking of toasts, and clashing of silver goblets.

At last when they had put away desire of eating and drinking, Iubdan rose up, having in his hand the royal goblet of gold inlaid with precious many-coloured jewels, and the heir-apparent rose at the other end of the table, and they drank prosperity and victory to Faylinn. Then Iubdan's heart swelled with pride, and he asked of the company, "Come now, have any of you ever seen a king more glorious and powerful than I am?" "Never, in truth," cried they all. "Have ye ever seen a stronger man than my giant, Glowar?" "Never, O King," said they. "Or battle-steeds and men-at-arms better than mine?" "By our words," they cried, "we never have." "Truly," went on Iubdan, "I deem that he who would assail our kingdom of Faylinn, and carry away captives and hostages from us, would have his work cut out for him, so fierce and mighty are our warriors; yea, any one of them hath the stuff of kingship in him."

On hearing this, Eisirt, in whom the heady wine and ale had done their work, burst out laughing; and the King turned to him, saying, "Eisirt, what hath moved thee to this laughter?" "I know a province in Erinn," replied Eisirt, "one man of whom would harry Faylinn in the teeth of all four battalions of the Wee Folk." "Seize him," cried the King to his attendants; "Eisirt shall pay dearly in chains and in prison for that scornful speech against our glory."

Then Eisirt was put in bonds, and he repented him of his brag; but ere they dragged him away he said, "Grant me, O mighty King, but three days' respite, that I may travel to Erinn to the court of Fergus mac Leda, and if I bring not back some clear token that I have uttered nought but the truth, then do with me as thou wilt."

So Iubdan bade them release him, and he fared away to Erinn oversea.

After this, one day, as Fergus and his lords sat at the feast, the gatekeeper of the palace of Fergus in Emania heard outside a sound of ringing; he opened the gate, and there stood a wee man holding in his hand a rod of white bronze hung with little silver bells, by which poets are wont to procure silence for their recitations. Most noble and comely was the little man to look on, though the short grass of the lawn reached as high as to his knee. His hair was twisted in four-ply strands after the manner of poets and he wore a gold-embroidered tunic of silk and an ample scarlet cloak with a fringe of gold. On his feet he wore shoes of white bronze ornamented with gold, and a silken hood was on his head. The gatekeeper wondered at the sight of the wee man, and went to report the matter to King Fergus. "Is he less," asked

Fergus, "than my dwarf and poet Æda?" "Verily," said the gatekeeper, "he could stand upon the palm of Æda's hand and have room to spare." Then with much laughter and wonder they all trooped out, lords and ladies, to the great gate to view the wee man and to speak with him. But Eisirt, when he saw them, waved them back in alarm, crying, "Avaunt, huge men; bring not your heavy breath so near me; but let yon man that is least among you approach me and bear me in". So the dwarf Æda put Eisirt on his palm and bore him into the banqueting hall.

Then they set him on the table, and Eisirt declared his name and calling. The King ordered that meat and drink should be given him, but Eisirt said, "I will neither eat of your meat nor drink of ale." "By our word," said Fergus, "'tis a haughty wight; he ought to be dropped into a goblet that he might at least drink all round him." The cupbearer seized Eisirt and put him into a tankard of ale, and he swam on the surface of it. "Ye wise men of Ulster," he cried, "there is much knowledge and wisdom ye might get from me, yet ye will let me be drowned!" "What, then?" cried they. Then Eisirt, beginning with the King, set out to tell every hidden sin that each man or woman had done, and ere he had gone far they with much laughter and chiding fetched him out of the ale-pot and dried him with fair satin napkins. "Now ye have confessed that I know somewhat to the purpose," said Eisirt, "and I will even eat of your food, but do ye give heed to my words, and do ill no more."

Fergus then said, "If thou art a poet, Eisirt, give us now a taste of thy delightful art." "That will I," said Eisirt, "and the poem that I shall recite to you shall be an ode in praise of my king, Iubdan the Great." Then he recited this lay:—

"A monarch of might
Is Iubdan my king.
His brow is snow-white,
His hair black as night;
As a red copper bowl
When smitten will sing,
So ringeth the voice
Of Iubdan the king.
His eyen, they roll
Majestic and bland
On the lords of his land
Arrayed for the fight,
A spectacle grand!
Like a torrent they rush
With a waving of swords
And the bridles all ringing
And cheeks all aflush,
And the battle-steeds springing,
A beautiful, terrible, death-dealing band.
Like pines, straight and tall,
Where Iubdan is king,
Are the men one and all.
The maidens are fair—
Bright gold is their hair.
From silver we quaff
The dark, heady ale
That never shall fail;
We love and we laugh.

Gold frontlets we wear;
And aye through the air
Sweet music doth ring—
O Fergus, men say
That in all Inisfail
There is not a maiden so proud or so wise
But would give her two eyes
Thy kisses to win—
But I tell thee, that there
Thou canst never compare
With the haughty, magnificent King of Faylinn!"

At this they all applauded, and Fergus said, "O youth and blameless bard, let us be friends henceforth."
And they all heaped before him, as a poet's reward, gifts of rings and jewels and gold cups and weapons,
as high as a tall man standing. Then Eisirt said, "Truly a generous and a worthy reward have ye given me,
O men of Ulster; yet take back these precious things I pray you, for every man in my king's household
hath an abundance of them." But the Ulster lords said, "Nothing that we have given may we take back."
Eisirt then bade two-thirds of his reward be given to the bards and learned men of Ulster, and one-third to
the horse-boys and jesters; and so it was done.

Three days and nights did Eisirt abide in Emania, and all the King's court loved him and made much of
him. Then he wished them blessing and victory, and prepared to depart to his own country. Now Æda, the
King's dwarf and minstrel, begged Eisirt to take him with him on a visit to the land of Faylinn; and Eisirt
said, "I shall not bid thee come, for then if kindness and hospitality be shown thee, thou wilt say it is only
what I had undertaken; but if thou come of thine own motion, thou wilt perchance be grateful."

So they went off together; but Eisirt could not keep up with Æda, and Æda said, "I perceive that Eisirt is
but a poor walker." At this Eisirt ran off like a flash and was soon an arrow flight in front of Æda. When
the latter at last came up with him, he said, "The right thing, Eisirt, is not too fast and not too slow."
"Since I have been in Ulster," Eisirt replied, "I have never before heard ye measure out the right."

By and by they reached the margin of the sea. "And what are we to do now?" asked Æda. "Be not
troubled, Æda," said Eisirt, "the horse of Iubdan will bear us easily over this." They waited awhile on the
beach, and ere long they saw it coming toward them skimming over the surface of the waves. "Save and
protect us!" cried Æda at that sight; and Eisirt asked him what he saw. "A red-maned hare," answered
Æda. "Nay, but that is Iubdan's horse," said Eisirt, and with that the creature came prancing to land with
flashing eyes and waving tail and a long russet-coloured mane; a bridle beset with gold it had. Eisirt
mounted and bade Æda come up behind him. "Thy boat is little enough for thee alone," said Æda. "Cease
fault-finding and grumbling," then said Eisirt, "for the weight of wisdom that is in thee will not bear him
down"

So Æda and Eisirt mounted on the fairy horse and away they sped over the tops of the waves and the
deeps of the ocean till at last they reached the Kingdom of Faylinn, and there were a great concourse of
the Wee Folk awaiting them. "Eisirt is coming! Eisirt is coming!" cried they all, "and a Fomorian giant
along with him."

Then Iubdan went forth to meet Eisirt, and he kissed him, and said, "Why hast thou brought this Fomorian
with thee to slay us?" "He is no Fomor," said Eisirt, "but a learned man and a poet from Ulster. He is
moreover the King of Ulster's dwarf, and in all that realm he is the smallest man. He can lie in their great
men's bosoms and stand upon their hands as though he were a child; yet for all that you would do well to

45

be careful how you behave to him." "What is his name?" said they then. "He is the poet Æda." said Eisirt. "Uch," said they, "what a giant thou hast brought us!"

"And now, O King," said Eisirt to Iubdan, "I challenge thee to go and see for thyself the region from which we have come, and make trial of the royal porridge which is made for Fergus King of Ulster this very night."

At this Iubdan was much dismayed, and he betook himself to Bebo his wife and told her how he was laid under bonds of chivalry by Eisirt to go to the land of the giants; and he bade her prepare to accompany him. "I will go," said she, "but you did an ill deed when you condemned Eisirt to prison."

So they mounted, both of them, on the fairy steed, and in no long time they reached Emania, and it was now past midnight. And they were greatly afraid, and said Bebo, "Let us search for that porridge and taste it, as we were bound, and make off again ere the folk awake."

They made their way into the palace of Fergus, and soon they found a great porridge pot, but the rim was too high to be reached from the ground. "Get thee up upon thy horse," said Bebo, "and from thence to the rim of this cauldron." And thus he did, but having gained the rim of the pot his arm was too short to reach the silver ladle that was in it. In straining downward to do so, however, he slipped and in he fell, and up to his middle in the thick porridge he stuck fast. And when Bebo heard what a plight he was in, she wept, and said, "Rash and hasty wert thou, Iubdan, to have got into this evil case, but surely there is no man under the sun that can make thee hear reason." And he said, "Rash indeed it was, but thou canst not help me, Bebo, now, and it is but folly to stay; take the horse and flee away ere the day break." "Say not so," replied Bebo, "for surely I will not go till I see how things fall out with thee."

At last the folk in the palace began to be stirring, and ere long they found Iubdan in the porridge pot.

So they picked him out with great laughter bore him off to Fergus.

"By my conscience," said Fergus, "but this is not the little fellow that was here before, for he had yellow hair, but this one hath a shock of the blackest; who art thou at all, wee man?"

"I am of the Wee Folk," said Iubdan, "and am indeed king over them, and this woman is my wife and queen, Bebo."

"Take him away," then said Fergus to his varlets, "and guard him well"; for he misdoubted some mischief of Faery was on foot.

"Nay, nay," cried Iubdan, "but let me not be with these coarse fellows. I pledge thee my word that I will not quit this place till thou and Ulster give me leave."

"Could I believe that," said Fergus, "I would not put thee in bonds."

"I have never broken my word," said Iubdan, "and I never will."

Then Fergus set him free and allotted him a fair chamber for himself, and a trusty servingman to wait upon him. Soon there came in a gillie whose business it was to see to the fires, and he kindled the fire for Iubdan, throwing on it a woodbine together with divers other sorts of timber. Then Iubdan said, "Man of smoke, burn not the king of the trees, for it is not meet to burn him. Wouldst thou but take counsel from me thou mightest go safely by sea or land." Iubdan then chanted to him the following recital of the duties of his office:—

"O fire-gillie of Fergus of the Feasts, never by land or sea burn the King of the woods, High King of the forests of Inisfail, whom none may bind, but who like a strong monarch holds all the other trees in hard bondage. If thou burn the twining one, misfortune will come of it, peril at the point of spear, or drowning in the waves.

"Burn not the sweet apple-tree of drooping branches, of the white blossoms, to whose gracious head each man puts forth his hand.

"The stubborn blackthorn wanders far and wide, the good craftsman burns not this timber; little though its bushes be, yet flocks of birds warble in them.

"Burn not the noble willow, the unfailing ornament of poems; bees drink from its blossoms, all delight in the graceful tent.

"The delicate, airy tree of the druids, the rowan with its berries, this burn; but avoid the weak tree, burn not the slender hazel.

"The ash-tree of the black buds burn not—timber that speeds the wheel, that yields the rider his switch; the ashen spear is the scale-beam of battle.

"The tangled, bitter bramble, burn him, the sharp and green; he flays and cuts the foot; he snares you and drags you back.

"Hottest of timber is the green oak; he will give you a pain in the head if you use him overmuch, a pain in the eyes will come from his biting fumes.

"Full-charged with witchcraft is the alder, the hottest tree in the fight; burn assuredly both the alder and the whitehorn at your will.

"Holly, burn it in the green and in the dry; of all trees in the world, holly is absolutely the best.

"The elder-tree of the rough brown bark, burn him to cinders, the steed of the Fairy Folk.

"The drooping birch, by all means burn him too, the tree of long-lasting bloom.

"And lay low, if it pleases you, the russet aspen; late or early, burn the tree with the quaking plumage.

"The yew is the venerable ancestor of the wood as the companion of feasts he is known; of him make goodly brown vats for ale and wine.

"Follow my counsel, O man of the smoke, and it shall go well with you, body and soul."

So Iubdan continued in Emania free to go and come as he pleased; and all the Ulstermen delighted to watch him and to hear his conversation.

One day it chanced that he was in the chamber of the Queen, and saw her putting on her feet a very dainty and richly embroidered pair of shoes. At this Iubdan gave a laugh. "Why dost thou laugh?" said Fergus. "Meseems the healing is applied very far from the hurt," replied Iubdan. "What meanest thou by that?" said Fergus. "Because the Queen is making her feet fine in order, O Fergus, that she may attract thee to her lips," said Iubdan.

Another time it chanced that Iubdan overheard one of the King's soldiers complaining of a pair of new brogues that had been served out to him, and grumbling that the soles were too thin. At this Iubdan laughed again, and being asked why, he said, "I must need laugh to hear yon fellow grumbling about his brogues, for the soles of these brogues, thin as they are, he will never wear out." And this was a true prophecy, for the same night this and another of the King's men had a quarrel, and fought, and killed each the other.

At last the Wee Folk determined to go in search of their king, and seven battalions of them marched upon Emania and encamped upon the lawn over against the King's Dún. Fergus and his nobles went out to confer with them. "Give us back our king," said the Wee Folk, "and we shall redeem him with a great ransom." "What ransom, then?" asked Fergus. "We shall," said they, "cause this great plain to stand thick with corn for you every year, and that without ploughing or sowing." "I will not give up Iubdan for that," said Fergus. "Then we shall do you a mischief," said the Wee Folk.

That night every calf in the Province of Ulster got access to its dam, and in the morn there was no milk to be had for man or child, for the cows were sucked dry.

Then said the Wee Folk to Fergus, "This night, unless we get Iubdan, we shall defile every well and lake and river in Ulster." "That is a trifle," said Fergus, "and ye shall not get Iubdan."

The Wee Folk carried out this threat, and once more they came and demanded Iubdan, saying, "To-night we shall burn with fire the shaft of every mill in Ulster." "Yet not so shall ye get Iubdan," said Fergus.

This being done, they came again, saying, "We shall have vengeance unless Iubdan be delivered to us" "What vengeance?" said Fergus. "We shall snip off every ear of corn in thy kingdom," said they. "Even so," replied Fergus, "I shall not deliver Iubdan."

So the Wee Folk snipped off every ear of standing corn in Ulster, and once more they returned and demanded Iubdan. "What will ye do next?" asked Fergus. "We shall shave the hair of every man and every woman in Ulster," said they, "so that ye shall be shamed and disgraced for ever among the people of Erinn." "By my word," said Fergus, "if ye do that I shall slay Iubdan."

Then Iubdan said, "I have a better counsel than that, O King; let me have liberty to go and speak with them, and I shall bid them make good what mischief they have done, and they shall return home forthwith."

Fergus granted that; and when the Wee Folk saw Iubdan approaching them, they set up a shout of triumph that a man might have heard a bowshot off, for they believed they had prevailed and that Iubdan was released to them. But Iubdan said, "My faithful people, you must now begone, and I may not go with you; make good also all the mischief that ye have done, and know that if ye do any more I must die."

Then the Wee Folk departed, very downcast and sorrowful, but they did as Iubdan had bidden them.

Iubdan, however, went to Fergus and said, "Take, O King, the choicest of my treasures, and let me go."

"What is thy choicest treasure?" said Fergus.

Iubdan then began to recite to Fergus the list of his possessions, such as druidic weapons, and love-charms, and instruments of music that played without touch of human hand, and vats of ale that could never be emptied; and he named among other noble treasures a pair of shoes, wearing which a man could go over or under the sea as readily as on dry land.

At the same time Æda, the dwarf and poet of Ulster, returned hale and well from the land of Faylinn, and much did he entertain the King and all the court with tales of the smallness of the Wee Folk, and their marvel at his own size, and their bravery and beauty, and their marble palaces and matchless minstrelsy.

So the King, Fergus mac Leda, was well content to take a ransom, namely the magic shoes, which he desired above all the treasures of Faylinn, and to let Iubdan go. And he gave him rich gifts, as did also the nobles of Ulster, and wished him blessing and victory; and Iubdan he departed, with Bebo his wife, having first bestowed upon Fergus the magical shoes. And of him the tale hath now no more to say.

But Fergus never tired of donning the shoes of Iubdan and traversing the secret depths of the lakes and rivers of Ulster. Thereby, too, in the end he got his death, for as the wise say that the gifts of Faery may not be enjoyed without peril by mortal men, so in this case too it proved. For, one day as Fergus was exploring the depths of Loch Rury he met the monster, namely the river-horse, which inhabited that lake. Horrible of form it was, swelling and contracting like a blacksmith's bellows, and with eyes like torches, and glittering tusks, and a mane of coarse hair on its crest and neck. When it saw Fergus it laid back its ears, and its neck arched like a rainbow over his head, and the vast mouth gaped to devour him. Then Fergus rose quickly to the surface and made for the land, and the beast after him, driving before it a huge wave of foam. Barely did he escape with his life; but with the horror of the sight his features were distorted and his mouth was twisted around to the side of his head, so that he was called Fergus Wry-mouth from that day forth. And the gillie that was with him told the tale of the adventure.

Now there was a law in Ireland that no man might be king who was disfigured by any bodily blemish. His people, therefore, loving Fergus, kept from him all knowledge of his condition, and the Queen let all mirrors that were in the palace be put away. But one day it chanced that a bondmaid was negligent in preparing the bath, and Fergus being impatient, gave her a stroke with a switch which he had in his hand. The maid in anger turned upon him, and cried, "It would better become thee to avenge thyself on the riverhorse that hath twisted thy mouth, than to do brave deeds on women."

Fergus then bade a mirror be fetched, and when he saw his face in it, he said, "The woman spake truth; the riverhorse of Loch Rury has done this thing."

The next day Fergus put on the shoes of Iubdan and went forth to Loch Rury, and with him went the lords of Ulster. And when he reached the margin of the lake he drew his sword and went down into it, and soon the waters covered him.

After a while those that watched upon the bank saw a bubbling and a mighty commotion in the waters, now here, now there, and waves of bloody froth broke at their feet. At last, as they strained their eyes upon the tossing water, they saw Fergus rise to his middle from it, pale and bloody. In his right hand he waved aloft his sword, his left was twisted in the coarse hair of the monster's head, and they saw that his countenance was fair and kingly as of old. "Ulstermen, I have conquered," he cried; and as he did so he sank down again, dead with his dead foe, into their red grave in Loch Rury.

And the Ulster lords went back to Emania, sorrowful yet proud, for they knew that a seed of honour had been sown that day in their land from which should spring a breed of high-hearted fighting men for many a generation to come.

CHAPTER V

The Carving of Mac Datho's Boar

Once upon a time there dwelt in the province of Leinster a wealthy hospitable lord named Mesroda, son of Datho. Two possessions had he; namely, a hound which could outrun every other hound and every wild beast in Erinn, and a boar which was the finest and greatest in size that man had ever beheld.

Now the fame of this hound was noised all about the land, and many were the princes and lords who longed to possess it. And it came to pass that Conor, King of Ulster, and Maev, Queen of Connacht, sent messengers to mac Datho to ask him to sell them the hound for a price, and both the messengers arrived at the Dún of mac Datho on the same day. Said the Connacht messenger, "We will give thee in exchange for the hound six hundred milch cows, and a chariot with two horses, the best that are to be found in Connacht, and at the end of a year thou shalt have as much again." And the messenger of King Conor said, "We will give no less than Connacht, and the friendship and alliance of Ulster, and that will be better for thee than the friendship of Connacht."

Then Mesroda mac Datho fell silent, and for three days he would not eat nor drink, nor could he sleep o' nights, but tossed restlessly on his bed. His wife observed his condition, and said to him, "Thy fast hath been long, Mesroda, though good food is by thee in plenty; and at night thou turnest thy face to the wall, and well I know thou dost not sleep. What is the cause of thy trouble?"

"There is a saying," replied mac Datho, "'Trust not a thrall with money, nor a woman with a secret.'"

"When should a man talk to a woman," said his wife, "but when something were amiss? What thy mind cannot solve perchance another's may."

Then mac Datho told his wife of the request for his hound both from Ulster and from Connacht at one and the same time, "and whichever of them I deny," he said, "they will harry my cattle and slay my people."

"Then hear my counsel," said the woman. "Give it to both of them, and bid them come and fetch it; and if there be any harrying to be done, let them even harry each other; but in no way mayest thou keep the hound."

On that, mac Datho rose up and shook himself, and called for food and drink, and made merry with himself and his guests. Then he sent privately for the messenger of Queen Maev, and said to him, "Long have I doubted what to do, but now I am resolved to give the hound to Connacht. Let ye send for it on such a day with a train of your nobles or warriors and bear him forth nobly and proudly, for he is worth it; and ye shall all have drink and food and royal entertainment in my Dún." So the messenger departed, well pleased.

To the Ulster messenger mac Datho said, "After much perplexity I have resolved to give my hound to Conor. Let the best of the Ulstermen come to fetch him, and they shall be welcomed and entertained as is fitting." And for these he named the same day as he had done for the embassy from Connacht.

When the appointed day came round, the flower of the fighting men of two provinces of Ireland were assembled before the Dún of the son of Datho, and there were also Conor, King of Ulster, and Ailill, the husband of Maev, Queen of Connacht. Mac Datho went forth to meet them. "Welcome, warriors," he said to them, "albeit for two armies at once we were not prepared." Then he bade them into the Dún, and in the great hall they sat down. Now in this hall there were seven doors, and between every two doors were benches for fifty men. Not as friends bidden to a feast did the men of Ulster and of Connacht look upon one another, since for three hundred years the provinces had ever been at war.

"Let the great boar be killed," said mac Datho, and it was done. For seven years had that boar been nourished on the milk of fifty cows; yet rather on venom should it have been nourished, such was the mischief that was to come from the carving of it.

When the boar was roasted it was brought in, and many other kinds of food as side dishes, "and if more be wanting to the feast," said mac Datho, "it shall be slain for you before the morning."

"The boar is good," said Conor.

"It is a fine boar," said Ailill; "and now, O mac Datho, how shall it be divided among us?"

There was among the Ulster company one Bricru, son of Carbad, whose delight was in biting speeches and in fomenting strife, though he himself was never known to draw sword in any quarrel. He now spoke from his couch in answer to Ailill:

"How should the boar be divided, O son of Datho, except by appointing to carve it him who is best in deeds of arms? Here be all the valiant men of Ireland assembled; have none of us hit each other a blow on the nose ere now?"

"Good," said Ailill, "so let it be done."

"We also agree," said Conor; "there are plenty of our lads in the house that have many a time gone round the border of the Provinces."

"You will want them to-night, Conor," said an old warrior from Conlad in the West. "They have often been seen on their backs on the roads of rushy Dedah, and many a fat steer have they left with me."

"It was a fat bullock thou didst have with thee once upon a day," replied Moonremar of Ulster, "even thine own brother, and by the rushy road of Conlad he came and went not back."

"'Twas a better man than he, even Irloth, son of Fergus mac Leda, who fell by the hand of Echbael in Tara Luachra," replied Lugad of Munster.

"Echbael?" cried Keltchar, son of Uthecar Hornskin of Ulster. "Is it of him ye boast, whom I myself slew and cut off his head?"

And thus the heroes bandied about the tales and taunts of their victories, until at length Ket, son of Maga of the Connachtmen, arose and stood over the boar and took the knife into his hand. "Now," he cried, "let one man in Ulster match his deeds with mine, or else hold ye your peace and let me carve the boar!"

For a while there was silence, and then Conor King of Ulster, said to Logary the Triumphant, "Stay that for me." So Logary arose and said, "Ket shall never carve the boar for all of us."

"Not so fast, Logary," said Ket. "It is the custom among you Ulstermen that when a youth first takes arms he comes to prove himself on us. So didst thou, Logary, and we met thee at the border. From that meeting I have thy chariot and horses, and thou hadst a spear through thy ribs Not thus wilt thou get the boar from me." Then Logary sat down on his bench.

"Ket shall never divide that pig," spake then a tall fair-haired warrior from Ulster, coming down the hall. "Whom have we here?" asked Ket. "A better man than thou," shouted the Ulstermen, "even Angus, son of Lama Gabad." "Indeed?" said Ket, "and why is his father called Lama Gabad [wanting a hand]?" "We know not," said they. "But I know it," said Ket. "Once I went on a foray to the East, and was attacked by a troop, Lama Gabad among them. He flung a lance at me. I seized the same lance and flung it back, and it shore off his hand, and it lay there on the field before him. Shall that man's son measure himself with me?" And Angus went to his bench and sat down.

"Keep up the contest," then cried Ket tauntingly, "or let me divide the boar." "That thou shalt not," cried another Ulster warrior of great stature. "And who is this?" said Ket. "Owen Mór, King of Fermag," said the Ulstermen. "I have seen him ere now," said Ket. "I took a drove of cattle from him before his own house. He put a spear through my shield and I flung it back and it tore out one of his eyes, and one-eyed he is to this day." Then Owen Mór sat down.

"Have ye any more to contest the pig with me?" then said Ket. "Thou hast not won it yet," said Moonremar, son of Gerrkind, rising up. "Is that Moonremar?" said Ket, "It is," they cried.

"It is but three days," said Ket, "since I was the last man who won renown of thee. Three heads of thy fighting men did I carry off from Dún Moonremar, and one of the three was the head of thy eldest son." Moonremar then sat down.

"Still the contest," said Ket, "or I shall carve the boar." "Contest thou shalt have," said Mend, son of Sword-heel. "Who is this?" said Ket. "'Tis Mend," cried all the Ulstermen.

"Shall the sons of fellows with nicknames come here to contend with me?" cried Ket. "I was the priest who christened thy father that name. 'Twas I who cut the heel off him, so that off he went with only one. What brings the son of that man to contend with me?" Mend then sat down in his seat.

"Come to the contest," said Ket, "or I shall begin to carve." Then arose from the Ulstermen a huge grey and terrible warrior. "Who is this?" asked Ket. "'Tis Keltcar, son of Uthecar," cried they all.

"Wait awhile, Keltcar," said Ket, "do not pound me to pieces just yet. Once, O Keltcar, I made a foray on thee and came in front of Dún. All thy folk attacked me, and thou amongst them. In a narrow pass we fought, and thou didst fling a spear at me and I at thee, but my spear went through thy loins and thou hast never been the better of it since." Then Keltcar sat down in his seat.

"Who else comes to the contest," cried Ket "or shall I at last divide the pig?" Up rose then the son of King Conor, named Cuscrid the Stammerer "Whom have we here?" said Ket. "'Tis Cuscrid son of Conor," cried they all. "He has the stuff of a king in him," said Ket. "No thanks to thee for that," said the youth.

"Well, then," said Ket, "thou madest thy first foray against us Connachtmen, and on the border of the Provinces we met thee. A third of thy people, thou didst leave behind thee, and came away with my spear through thy throat, so that thou canst not speak rightly ever since, for the sinews of thy throat were severed. And hence is Cuscrid the Stammerer thy byname ever since."

So thus Ket laid shame and defeat on the whole Province of Ulster, nor was there any other warrior in the hall found to contend with him.

Then Ket stood up triumphing, and took the knife in his hand and prepared to carve the boar when a noise and trampling were heard at the great door of the hall, and a mighty shout of exultation arose from the Ulstermen. When the press parted, Ket saw coming up the centre of the hall Conall of the Victories, and Conor the King dashed the helmet from his head and sprang up for joy.

"Glad we are," cried Conall, "that all is ready for feast; and who is carving the boar for us?"

"Ket, son of Maga," replied they, "for none could contest the place of honour with him."

"Is that so, Ket?" says Conall Cearnach.

"Even so," replied Ket. "And now welcome to thee, O Conall, thou of the iron heart and fiery blood; keen as the glitter of ice, ever-victorious chieftain; hail mighty son of Finnchoom!"

And Conall said, "Hail to thee, Ket, flower of heroes, lord of chariots, a raging sea in battle; a strong, majestic bull; hail, son of Maga!"

"And now," went on Conall, "rise up from the boar and give me place."

"Why so?" replied Ket.

"Dost thou seek a contest from me?" said Conall; "verily thou shalt have it. By the gods of my nation I swear that since I first took weapons in my hand I have never passed one day that I did not slay a Connachtman, nor one night that I did not make a foray on them, nor have I ever slept but I had the head of a Connachtman under my knee."

"I confess," then, said Ket, "that thou art a better man than I, and I yield thee the boar. But if Anluan my brother were here, he would match thee deed for deed, and sorrow and shame it is that he is not."

"Anluan is here," shouted Conall, and with that he drew from his girdle the head of Anluan and dashed it in the face of Ket.

Then all sprang to their feet and a wild shouting and tumult arose, and the swords flew out of themselves, and battle raged in the hall of mac Datho. Soon the hosts burst out through the doors of the Dún and smote and slew each other in the open field, until the Connacht host were put to flight. The hound of mac Datho pursued them along with the Ulstermen, and it came up with the chariot in which King Ailill was driving, and seized the pole of the chariot, but the charioteer dealt it a blow that cut off its head. When

Ailill drew rein they found the hound's head still clinging to the pole, whence that place is called Ibar Cinn Chon, or the Yew Tree of the Hound's Head.

Now when Conor pursued hard upon King Ailill, Ferloga, the charioteer of Ailill, lighted down and hid himself in the heather; and as Conor drove past, Ferloga leaped up behind him in the chariot and gripped him by the throat.

"What will thou have of me?" said Conor.

"Give over the pursuit," said Ferloga, "and take me with thee to Emania,[19] and let the maidens of Emania so long as I am there sing a serenade before my dwelling every night."

"Granted," said Conor. So he took Ferloga with him to Emania, and at the end of a year sent him back to Connacht, escorting him as far as to Athlone; and Ferloga had from the King of Ulster two noble horses with golden bridles, but the serenade from the maidens of Ulster he did not get, though he got the horses instead. And thus ends the tale of the contention between Ulster and Connacht over the Carving of mac Datho's Boar.

CHAPTER VI

The Vengeance of Mesgedra

Atharna the Bard, surnamed the Extortionate, was the chief poet and satirist of Ulster in the reign of Conor mac Nessa. Greed and arrogance were in his heart and poison on his tongue, and the kings and lords of whom he asked rewards for his poems dared not refuse him aught, partly because of the poisonous satires and lampoons which he would otherwise make upon them for their niggardliness, and partly for that in Ireland at that day it was deemed shameful to refuse to a bard whatsoever he might ask. Once it was said that he asked of a sub-king, namely Eochy mac Luchta, who was famed for hospitality and generosity, the single thing that Eochy would have been grieved to give, namely his eye, and Eochy had but one eye. But the King plucked it out by the roots and gave it to him; and Atharna went away disappointed, for he had looked that Eochy would ransom his eye at a great price.

Now Conor mac Nessa, King of Ulster, and all the Ulster lords, having grown very powerful and haughty, became ill neighbours to all the other kingdoms in Ireland. On fertile Leinster above all they fixed their eyes, and sought for an opportunity to attack and plunder the province. Conor resolved at last to move Atharna to go to the King of Leinster, in the hope that he himself might be rid of Atharna, by the King of Leinster killing him for his insolence and his exactions, and that he might avenge the death of his bard by the invasion of Leinster.

Atharna therefore set out for Leinster accompanied by his train of poets and harpers and gillies and arrived at the great Dún of Mesgedra the King, at Naas in Kildare. Here he dwelt for twelve months wasting the substance of the Leinstermen and in the end when he was minded to return to Ulster he went before the King Mesgedra and the lords of Leinster and demanded his poet's fee.

"What is thy demand, Atharna?" asked Mesgedra.

"So many cattle and so many sheep," answered Atharna, "and store of gold and raiment, and of the fairest dames and maidens of Leinster forty-five, to grind at my querns in Dún Atharna."

"It shall be granted thee," said the King. Then Atharna feared some mischief, for the King and the nobles of Leinster had not seemed like men on whom shameful conditions are laid, nor had they offered to ransom their women. Atharna therefore judged that the Leinstermen might fall upon him to recover their booty when he was once beyond the border, for within their own borders they might not affront a guest. He sent, therefore, a swift messenger to Conor mac Nessa, bidding him come with a strong escort as quickly as he might, to meet Atharna's band on the marches of Leinster, and convey him safely home.

Atharna then departed from Naas with a great herd of sheep and cattle and other spoils, and with thrice fifteen of the noble women of Leinster. He went leisurely, meaning to strike the highroad to Emania from Dublin; but when he came thither the Liffey was swollen with rain, and the ford at Dublin might not be crossed. He caused, therefore, many great hurdles to be made, and these were set in the river, and over them a causeway of boughs was laid, so that his cattle and spoils came safely across. Hence is the town of that place called to this day in Gaelic the City of the Hurdle Ford.

On the next day Conor and the Ulstermen met him, but a great force of the men of Leinster was also marching from Naas to the border, to recover their womenfolk, even as Atharna had expected. The Leinstermen then broke the battle on the company from Ulster, and defeated them, driving them with the cows of Atharna on to the sea cape of Ben Edar (Howth), but they recovered the women. On Ben Edar did King Conor with the remnant of his troop then fortify themselves, making a great fosse across the neck of land by which Ben Edar is joined to the mainland, and here they were besieged, with hard fighting by day and night, expecting that help should come to them from Ulster, whither they had sent messengers to tell of their distress.

Now Conall of the Victories was left behind to rule in Emania when Conor set forth to Leinster, and he now, on hearing how the King was beset, assembled a great host and marched down to Ben Edar. Here he attacked the host of Leinster, and a great battle was fought, many being slain on both sides, and the King of Leinster, Mesgedra, lost his left hand in the fight. In the end the men of Leinster were routed, and fled, and Mesgedra drove in his chariot past the City of the Hurdle Ford and Naas to the fords of Liffey at Clane. Here there was a sacred oak tree where druid rites and worship were performed, and that oak tree was sanctuary, so that within its shadow, guarded by mighty spells, no man might be slain by his enemy.

Now Conall Cearnach had followed hard on the track of Mesgedra, and when he found him beneath the oak, he drove his chariot round and round the circuit of the sanctuary, bidding Mesgedra come forth and do battle with him, or be counted a dastard among the kings of Erinn. But Mesgedra said, "Is it the fashion of the champions of Ulster to challenge one-armed men to battle?"

Then Conall let his charioteer bind one of his arms to his side, and again he taunted Mesgedra and bade him come forth.

Mesgedra then drew sword, and between him and Conall there was a fierce fight until the Liffey was reddened with their blood. At last, by a chance blow of the sword of Mesgedra, the bonds of Conall's left arm were severed.

"On thy head be it," said Conall, "if thou release me again."

Then he caused his arm to be bound up once more, and again they met, sword to sword, and again in the fury of the fight Mesgedra cut the thongs that bound Conall's arm. "The gods themselves have doomed thee," shouted Conall then, and he rushed upon Mesgedra and in no long time he wounded him to death.

"Take my head," said Mesgedra then, "and add my glory to thy glory, but be well assured this wrong shall yet be avenged by me upon Ulster," and he died.

Then Conall cut off the head of Mesgedra and put it in his chariot, and took also the chariot of Mesgedra and fared northwards. Ere long he met a chariot and fifty women accompanying it. In it was Buan the Queen, wife of Mesgedra, returning from a visit to Meath.

"Who art thou, woman?" said Conall.

"I am Buan, wife of Mesgedra the King."

"Thou art to come with me," then said Conall.

"Who hath commanded this?" said Buan.

"Mesgedra the King," said Conall.

"By what token dost thou lay these commands upon me?"

"Behold his chariot and his horses," said Conall.

"He gives rich gifts to many a man," answered the Queen.

Then Conall showed her the head of her husband.

"This is my token," said he.

"It is enough," said Buan. "But give me leave to bewail him ere I go into captivity."

Then Buan rose up in her chariot and raised for Mesgedra a keen of sorrow so loud and piercing that her heart broke with it, and she fell backwards on the road and died.

Conall Cearnach then buried her there, and laid the head of her husband by her side; and the fair hazel tree that grew from her grave by the fords of Clane was called Coll Buana, or the Hazel Tree of Buan.

But ere Conall buried the head of Mesgedra he caused the brain to be taken out and mixed with lime to make a bullet for a sling, for so it was customary to do when a great warrior had been killed; and the brain-balls thus made were accounted to be the deadliest of missiles.

So when Leinster had been harried and plundered and its king and queen thus slain, the Ulstermen drew northward again, and the brain-ball was laid up in the Dún of King Conor at Emania.

Years afterwards it happened that the Wolf of Connacht, namely Ket, son of Maga, came disguised within the borders of Ulster in search of prey, and he entered the palace precincts of Conor in Emania. There he saw two jesters of the King, who had gotten the brain-ball from the shelf where it lay, and were rolling it

56

about the courtyard. Ket knew it for what it was, and put it out of sight of the jesters and took it away with him while they made search for it. Thenceforth Ket carried it ever about with him in his girdle, hoping that he might yet use it to destroy some great warrior among the Ulstermen.

One day thereafter Ket made a foray on the men of Ross, and carried away a spoil of cattle. The host of Ulster and King Conor with them overtook him as he went homeward. The men of Connacht had also mustered to the help of Ket, and both sides made them ready for battle.

Now a river, namely Brosna, ran between them, and on a hill at one side of this were assembled a number of the noble women of Connacht, who desired greatly to look on the far-famed Ultonian warriors, and above all on Conor the King, whose presence was said to be royal and stately beyond any man that was then living in Erinn. Among the bushes, close to the women, Ket hid himself, and lay still but watchful.

Now Conor, seeing none but womenfolk close to him at this point, and being willing to show them his splendour, drew near to the bank on his side of the stream. Then Ket leaped up, whirling his sling, and the bullet hummed across the river and smote King Conor on the temple. And his men carried him off for dead, and the men of Connacht broke the battle on the Ulstermen, slaying many, and driving the rest of them back to their own place. This battle was thenceforth called the Battle of the Ford of the Sling-cast, or Athnurchar; and so the place is called to this day.

When Conor was brought home to Emania his chief physician, Fingen, found the ball half buried in his temple. "If the ball be taken out," said Fingen, "he will die; if it remain he will live, but he will bear the blemish of it."

"Let him bear the blemish," said the Ulster lords, "that is a small matter compared with the death of Conor."

Then Fingen stitched the wound over with a thread of gold, for Conor had curling golden hair, and bade him keep himself from all violent movements and from all vehement passions, and not to ride on horseback, and he would do well.

After that Conor lived for seven years, and he went not to war during that time, and all cause of passion was kept far from him. Then one day at broad noon the sky darkened, and the gloom of night seemed to spread over the world, and all the people feared, and looked for some calamity. Conor called to him his chief druid, namely Bacarach, and inquired of him as to the cause of the gloom.

The druid then went with Conor into a sacred grove of oaks and performed the rites of divination, and in a trance he spoke to Conor, saying, "I see a hill near a great city, and three high crosses on it. To one of them is nailed the form of a young man who is like unto one of the Immortals. Round him stand soldiers with tall spears, and a great crowd waiting to see him die."

"Is he, then, a malefactor?"

"Nay," said the druid, "but holiness, innocence, and truth have come to earth in him, and for this cause have the druids of his land doomed him to die, for his teaching was not as theirs. And the heavens are darkened for wrath and sorrow at the sight."

Then Conor leaped up in a fury, crying, "They shall not slay him, they shall not slay him! Would I were there with the host of Ulster, and thus would I scatter his foes"; and with that he snatched his sword and began striking at the trees that stood thickly about him in the druid grove. Then with the heat of his passion the sling-ball burst from his head, and he fell to the ground and died.

Thus was fulfilled the vengeance of Mesgedra upon Conor mac Nessa, King of Ulster.

CHAPTER VII

The Story of Etain and Midir

Once upon a time there was a High King of the Milesian race in Ireland named Eochy Airem, whose power and splendour were very great, and all the sub-Kings, namely, Conor of Ulster, and Mesgedra of Leinster, and Curoi of Munster, and Ailill and Maev of Connacht, were obedient to him. But he was without a wife; and for this reason the sub-Kings and Princes of Ireland would not come to his festivals at Tara, "for," said they, "there is no noble in Ireland who is a wifeless man, and a King is no king without a queen." And they would not bring their own wives to Tara without a queen there to welcome them, nor would they come themselves and leave their womenfolk at home.

So Eochy bade search be made through all the boundaries of Ireland for a maiden meet to be wife of the High King. And in time his messengers came back and said that they had found in Ulster, by the Bay of Cichmany, the fairest and most accomplished maiden in Ireland, and her name was Etain, daughter of Etar, lord of the territory called Echrad. So Eochy, when he had heard their report, went forth to woo the maiden.

When he drew near his journey's end he passed by a certain spring of pure water where it chanced that Etain and her maids had come down that she might wash her hair. She held in her hand a comb of silver inlaid with gold, and before her was a bason of silver chased with figures of birds, and around the rim of it red carbuncles were set. Her mantle was purple with a fringe of silver, and it was fastened with a broad golden brooch. She wore also a tunic of green silk, stiff with embroidery ofgold that glittered in the sun. Her hair before she loosed it was done in two mighty tresses, yellow like the flower of the waterflag, each tress being plaited in four strands, and at the end of each strand a little golden ball. When she laid aside her mantle her arms came through the armholes of her tunic, white as the snow of a single night, and her cheeks were ruddy as the foxglove. Even and small were her teeth, as if a shower of pearls had fallen in her mouth. Her eyes were hyacinth-blue, her lips scarlet as the rowan-berry, her shoulders round and white, her fingers were long and her nails smooth and pink. Her feet also were slim, and white as sea-foam. The radiance of the moon was in her face, pride in her brows, the light of wooing in her eyes. Of her it was said that there was no beauty among women compared with Etain's beauty, no sweetness compared with the sweetness of Etain.

When the King saw her his heart burned with love for her, and when he had speech with her he besought her to be his bride. And she consented to that, and said, "Many have wooed me, O King, but I would none of them, for since I was a little child I have loved thee, for the high tales that I heard of thee and of thy glory." And Eochy said, "Thine alone will I be if thou wilt have me." So the King paid a great bride-price for her, and bore her away to Tara, and there they were wedded, and all men welcomed and honoured the Queen. Nor had she dwelt long in Tara before the enchantment of her beauty and her grace had worked upon the hearts of all about her, so that the man to whom she spoke grew pale at the womanly sweetness of her voice, and felt himself a king for that day. All fair things and bright she loved, such as racing steeds and shining raiment, and the sight of Eochy's warriors with their silken banners and shields decorated

58

with rich ornament in red and blue. And she would have all about her happy and joyous, and she gave freely of her treasure, and of her smiles and loving words, if she might see the light of joy on the faces of men, but from pain or sadness that might not be cured she would turn away. In one thing only was sadness endurable to her and that was in her music, for when she sang or touched the harp all hearts were pierced with longing for they knew not what, and all eyes shed tears save hers alone, who looked as though she beheld, far from earth, some land more fair than words of man can tell; and all the wonder of that land and all its immeasurable distance were in her song.

Now Eochy the King had a brother whose name was Ailill Anglounach, or Ailill of the Single Stain, for one dark spot only was on his life, and it is of this that the story now shall tell. One day, when he had come from his own Dún to the yearly Assembly in the great Hall of Tara, he ate not at the banquet but gazed as it were at something afar off, and his wife said to him, "Why dost thou gaze so, Ailill; so do men look who are smitten with love?" Ailill was wroth with himself and turned his eyes away, but he said nothing, for that on which he gazed was the face of Etain.

After that Assembly was over Ailill knew that the torment of love had seized him for his brother's wife, and he was sorely shamed and wrathful, and the secret strife in his mind between his honour and the fierce and pitiless love that possessed him brought him into a sore sickness. And he went home to his Dún in Tethba and there lay ill for a year. Then Eochy the King went to see him, and came near him and laid his hand on his breast, and Ailill heaved a bitter sigh. Eochy asked, "Why art thou not better of this sickness, how goes it with thee now?" "By my word," said Ailill, "no better, but worse each day and night." "What ails thee, then?" asked Eochy. Ailill said, "Verily, I know not." Then Eochy bade summon his chief physician, who might discover the cause of his brother's malady, for Ailill was wasting to death.

So Fachtna the chief physician came and he laid his hand upon Ailill, and Ailill sighed. Then Fachtna said, "This is no bodily disease, but either Ailill suffers from the pangs of envy or from the torment of love." But Ailill was full of shame and he would not tell what ailed him, and Fachtna went away.

After this the time came that Eochy the High King should make a royal progress throughout his realm of Ireland, but Etain he left behind at Tara. Before he departed he charged her saying, "Do thou be gentle and kind to my brother Ailill while he lives, and should he die, let his burial mound be heaped over him, and a pillar stone set up above it, and his name written thereon in letters of Ogham." Then the King took leave of Ailill and looked to see him again on earth no more.

After a while Etain bethought her and said, "Let us go to see how it fares with Ailill." So she went to where he lay in his Dún at Tethba. And seeing him wasted and pale she was moved with pity and distress and said,

"What ails thee, young man? Long thou hast lain prostrate, in fair weather and in foul, thou who wert wont to be so swift and strong?"

And Ailill said,

"Truly, I have a cause for my suffering; and I cannot eat, nor listen to the music makers; my affliction is very sore."

Then said Etain,

"Though I am a woman I am wise in many a thing; tell me what ails thee and thy healing shall be done."

59

Ailill replied,

"Blessing be with thee, O fair one; I am not worthy of thy speech; I am torn by the contention of body and of soul."

Then Etain deemed that she knew somewhat of his trouble, and she said,

"If thy heart is set on any of the white maidens that are my handmaids, tell me of it, and I shall court her for thee and she shall come to thee," and then Ailill cried out,

"Love indeed, O Queen, hath brought me low. It is a plague nearer than the skin, it overwhelms my soul as an earthquake, it is farther than the height of the sky, and harder to win than the treasures of the Fairy Folk. If I contend with it, it is like a combat with a spectre; if I fly to the ends of the earth from it, it is there; if I seek to seize it, it is a passion for an echo. It is thou, O my love, who hast brought me to this, and thou alone canst heal me, or I shall never rise again."

Then Etain went away and left him. But still in her palace in Tara she was haunted by his passion and his misery, and, though she loved him not, she could not endure his pain, nor the triumph of grim death over his youth and beauty. So at last she went to him again and said, "If it lies with me, Ailill, to heal thee of thy sickness, I may not let thee die." And she made a tryst to meet him on the morrow at a house of Ailill's between Dún Tethba and Tara, "but be it not at Tara," she said, "for that is the palace of the High King."

All that night Ailill lay awake with the thought of his tryst with Etain. But on the morrow morn a heaviness came upon his eyelids, and a druid sleep overcame him, and there all day he lay buried in slumbers from which none could wake him, until the time of his meeting with Etain was overpast.

But Etain, when she had come to the place of the tryst, looked out, and behold, a youth having the appearance and the garb of Ailill was approaching from Tethba. He entered the bower where she was; but no lover did she there meet, but only a sick and sorrowful man who spake coldly to her and lamented the sufferings of his malady, and after a short time he went away.

Next day Etain went to see Ailill and to hear how he did. And Ailill entreated her forgiveness that he had not kept his tryst, "for," said he, "a druid slumber descended upon me, and I lay as one dead from morn till eve. And morever," he added, "it seems as if the strange passion that has befallen me were washed away in that slumber, for now, Etain, I love thee no more but as my Queen and my sister, and I am recovered as if from an evil dream." Then Etain knew that powers not of earth were mingling in her fate, and she pondered much of these things, and grew less lighthearted than of old. And when the King came back, he rejoiced to find his brother whole and sound and merry, as Ailill had ever been, and he praised Etain for her gentleness and care.

Now after a time as Etain was by herself in her sunny bower she was aware of a man standing by her, whom she had never seen before. Young he was, and grey-eyed, with curling golden hair, and in his hand he bore two spears. His mantle was of crimson silk, his tunic of saffron, and a golden helmet was on his head. And as she gazed upon him, "Etain," he said, "the time is come for thee to return; we have missed thee and sorrowed for thee long enough in the Land of Youth." Etain said, "Of what land dost thou speak?" Then he chanted to her a song:—

"Come with me, Etain, O come away,
To that oversea land of mine! Where music haunts the happy day,

And rivers run with wine; Where folk are careless, and young, and gay,
And none saith 'mine' or 'thine.'

"Golden curls on the proud young head,
And pearls in the tender mouth; Manhood, womanhood, white and red,
And love that grows not loth When all the world's desires are dead,
And all the dreams of youth.

"Away from the cloud of Adam's sin!
Away from grief and care! This flowery land thou dwellest in
Seems rude to us, and bare; For the naked strand of the Happy Land
Is twenty times as fair."

When Etain heard this she stood motionless and as one that dreams awake, for it seemed to her as if she must follow that music whithersoever it went on earth or beyond the earth. But at last remembrance came upon her and she said to the stranger, "Who art thou, that I, the High King's wife, should follow a nameless man and betray my troth?" And he said, "Thy troth was due to me before it was due to him, and, moreover, were it not for me thou hadst broken it already. I am Midir the Proud, a prince among the people of Dana, and thy husband, Etain. Thus it was, that when I took thee to wife in the Land of Youth, the jealousy of thy rival, Fuamnach, was awakened; and having decoyed me from home by a false report, she changed thee by magical arts into a butterfly and then contrived a mighty tempest that drove thee abroad. Seven years wast thou borne hither and thither on the blast till chance blew thee into the fairy palace of Angus my kinsman, by the waters of the Boyne. But Angus knew thee, for the Fairy Folk may not disguise themselves from each other, and he built for thee a magical sunny bower with open windows, through which thou mightest pass, and about it were all manner of blossoming herbs and shrubs, and on the odour and honey of these thou didst live and grow fair and well nourished. But in the end Fuamnach got tidings of thee, and again the druid tempest descended and blew thee forth for another seven years of wandering and woe. Then it chanced that thou wert blown through the roof-window of the Dún of Etar by the Bay of Cichmany, and fell into the goblet from which his wife was drinking, and thee she drank down with that draught of ale. And in due time thou wast born again in the guise of a mortal maid and daughter to Etar the Warrior. But thou art no mortal, nor of mortal kin, for it is one thousand and twelve years from the time when thou wast born in Fairy Land till Etar's wife bore thee as a child on earth."

Then Etain was bewildered, and her mind ran back on many a half-forgotten thing and she gazed as into a gulf of visions, full of dim shapes, strange and glorious. And Midir as she looked at him again seemed transfigured, taller and mightier than before, and a light flame flickered from his helmet's crest and moved like wings about his shoulders.

But at last she said, "I know not what thou sayest if it be truth or not, but this I know, that I am the wife of the High King and I will not break my troth." "It were broken already," said Midir, "but for me, for I it was who laid a druidic sleep on Ailill, and it was I who came to thee in his shape that thy honour might not be stained." Etain said, "I learned then that honour is more than life." "But if Eochy the High King consent to let thee go," said Midir, "wilt thou then come with me to my land and thine?" "In that case," said Etain "I will go."

And the time went by, and Etain abode in Tara, and the High King did justice and made war and held the great Assembly as he was used. But one day in summer Eochy arose very early to breathe the morning air, and he stood by himself leaning on the rampart of his great Dún, and looking over the flowery plain of Bregia. And as he thus gazed he was aware of a young warrior standing by his side. Grey-eyed the youth was, and golden-haired, and he was splendidly armed and apparelled as beseemed the lord of a great clan of the Gael. Eochy bade him welcome courteously, and asked him of the cause of his coming. "I am come," he said, "to play a game of chess with thee, O King, for thou art renowned for thy skill in that game, and to test that skill am I come. And my name is Midir, of the People of Dana, whom they have called The Proud."

"Willingly," said the King; "but I have here no chessboard, and mine is in the chamber where the Queen is sleeping."

"That is easily remedied," said Midir, and he drew from his cloak a folding chessboard whose squares were alternate gold and silver. From a men-bag made of brazen chainwork he drew out a set of men adorned with flashing jewels, and he set them in array.

"I will not play," then said Eochy, "unless we play for a stake."

"For what stake shall we play, then?" said Midir.

"I care not," said Eochy; "but do thou perform tasks for me if I win and I shall bestow of my treasures upon thee if I lose."

So they played a game, and Eochy won. Then Eochy bade Midir clear the plains of Meath about Tara from rocks and stones, and Midir brought at night a great host of the Fairy Folk, and it was done. And again he played with Eochy, and again he lost, and this time he cut down the forest of Breg. The third time Midir lost again, and his task was to build a causeway across the moor of Lamrach. Now at night, while Midir and the fairy host were labouring at the causeway and their oxen drawing to it innumerable loads of earth and gravel, the steward of Eochy stole out and hid himself to watch them, for it was a prohibition to see them at work. And he observed that the fairy oxen were not harnessed with a thong across their foreheads, that the pull might be upon their brows and necks, as was the manner with the Gael, but with yokes upon their shoulders. This he reported to Eochy, who found it good; and he ordered that henceforth the children of the Gael should harness their plough-oxen with the yoke upon their shoulders; and so it was done from that day forth. Hence Eochy got his name of *Airem*, or "The Ploughman," for he was the first of the Gael to put the yoke upon the shoulder of the ox.

But it was said that because the Fairy Folk were watched as they made that noble causeway, there came a breach in it at one place which none could ever rightly mend.

When all their works were accomplished, Midir came again to Eochy, and this time he bore a dark and fierce countenance and was high girt as for war. And the King welcomed him, and Midir said, "Thou hast treated me hardly and put slavish tasks upon me. All that seemed good to thee have I done, but now I am moved with anger against thee."

"I return not anger for anger," said Eochy; "say what satisfaction I can make thee."

"Let us once more play at chess," said Midir.

"Good," said Eochy, "and what stake wilt thou have now?"

"The stake to be whatever the winner shall demand," said Midir.

Then they played for the fourth time and Eochy lost.

"Thou hast won the game," said he.

"I had won long ago had I chosen," said Midir.

"What dost thou demand of me?" said Eochy.

"To hold Etain in my arms and obtain a kiss from her," replied Midir.

The King was silent for a while and after that he said, "Come back in one month from this day and the stake which I have lost shall be paid."

But Eochy summoned together all the host of the heroes of the Gael, and they surrounded Tara, ring within ring; and the King himself and Etain were in the palace, with the outer court of it shut and locked. For they looked that Midir should come with a great host of the Danaan folk to carry off the Queen. And on the appointed day, as the kings sat at meat, Etain and her handmaids were dispensing the wine to them as was wont. Then suddenly as they feasted and talked, behold, Midir, stood in the midst of them. If he was fair and noble to look on as he had appeared before to the King and to Etain, he was fairer now, for the splendour of the Immortals clothed him, and his jewels flamed as he moved like eyes of living light. And all the kings and lords and champions who were present gazed on him in amazement and were silent, as the King arose and gave him welcome.

"Thou hast received me as I expected to be received," said Midir, "and now let thy debt be paid, since I for my part faithfully performed all that I undertook."

"I must consider the matter yet longer," said Eochy.

"Thou hast promised Etain's very self to me," said Midir; "that is what hath come from thee." And when she heard that word Etain blushed for shame.

"Blush not," said Midir, "for all the treasures of the Land of Youth have not availed to win thee from Eochy, and it is not of thine own will that thou art won, but because the time is come to return to thy kin."

Then said Eochy, "I have not promised Etain's self to thee, but to take her in thine arms and kiss her, and now do so if thou wilt."

Then Midir took his weapons in his left hand and placed his right around Etain, and when he did so they rose up in the air over the heads of the host, and passed through a roof-window in the palace. Then all rose up, tumultuous and angry, and rushed out of doors, but nothing could they see save two white swans that circled high in air around the Hill of Tara, and then flew southwards and away towards the fairy mountain of Slievenamon. And thus Etain the immortal rejoined the Immortals; but a daughter of Etain and of Eochy, who was another Etain in name and in beauty, became in due time a wife, and mother of kings.

CHAPTER VIII

How Ethne Quitted Fairyland

By the banks of the River Boyne, where rises the great Fairy Mound now called Newgrange, there stood long ago the shining Palace of a prince of the People of Dana, named Angus. Of him it is that the lines are written—

"By the dark rolling waters of the Boyne
Where Angus Óg magnificently dwells."

When the Milesian race invaded Ireland, and after long fighting subdued the Danaans in spite of all their enchantments and all their valour, the Danaans wrought for themselves certain charms by which they and all their possessions became invisible to mortals, and thus they continued to lead their old joyous life in the holy places of the land, and their palaces and dancing-places and folk-motes seem to the human eye to be merely a green mound or rath, or a lonely hillside, or a ruined shrine with nettles and foxgloves growing up among its broken masonry.

Now, after Angus and his folk had thus retreated behind the veil of invisibility, it happened that the steward of his palace had a daughter born to him whose name was Ethne. On the same day Fand, the wife of Mananan the Sea God, bore him a daughter, and since Angus was a friend of Mananan and much beloved by him, the child of the Sea God was sent to Brugh na Boyna, the noble dwelling-place of Angus, to be fostered and brought up, as the custom was. And Ethne became the handmaid of the young princess of the sea.

In time Ethne grew into a fair and stately maiden Now in the Brugh of Angus there were two magical treasures, namely, an ale-vat which could never be emptied, and two swine whereof one was ever roasted and ready to be eaten while the other lived, and thus they were, day and day about. There was therefore always a store of food of faery, charged with magical spells, by eating of which one could never grow old or die. It came to be noticed that after Ethne had grown up she never ate or drank of the fairy food, or of any other, yet she continued to seem healthy and well-nourished. This was reported to Angus, and by him to Mananan, and Mananan by his wisdom discovered the cause of it. One of the lords of the Danaans, happening to be on a visit with Angus, was rendered distraught by the maiden's beauty, and one day he laid hands upon her and strove to carry her away to his own dwelling. Ethne escaped from him, but the blaze of resentment at the insult that lit up in her soul consumed in her the fairy nature, that knows not of good or evil, and the nature of the children of Adam took its place. Thenceforth she ate not of the fairy food, which is prohibited to man, and she was nourished miraculously by the will of the One God. But after a time it chanced that Mananan and Angus brought from the Holy Land two cows whose milk could never run dry. In this milk there was nothing of the fairy spell, and Ethne lived upon it many long years, milking the cows herself, nor did her youth and beauty suffer any change.

Now it happened that on one very hot day the daughter of Mananan went down to bathe in the waters of the Boyne, and Ethne and her other maidens along with her. After they had refreshed themselves in the cool, amber-coloured water, they arrayed themselves in their silken robes and trooped back to the Brugh again; but ere they entered it, they discovered that Ethne was not among them.

So they went back, scattering themselves along the bank and searching in every quiet pool of the river and in every dark recess among the great trees that bordered it, for Ethne was dearly loved by all of them; but neither trace nor tidings of her could they find, and they went sorrowfully home without her, to tell the tale to Angus and to her father.

What had befallen Ethne was this. In taking off her garments by the riverside she had mislaid her fairy charm, and was become as a mortal maid. Nothing could she now see of her companions, and all around was strange to her. The fairy track that had led to the riverside was overgrown with briars, the palace of Angus was but a wooded hill. She knew not where she was, and pierced with sudden terror she fled wildly away, seeking for the familiar places that she had known in the fairy life, but which were now behind the Veil. At length she came to a high wall wherein was a wicket gate, and through it she saw a garden full of sweet herbs and flowers, which surrounded a steep-roofed building of stone. In the garden she saw a man in a long brown robe tied about his waist with a cord. He smiled at her and beckoned her to come in without fear. He was a monk of the holy Patrick, and the house was a convent church.

When the monk had heard her tale, he marvelled greatly and brought her to St Patrick himself, who instructed her in the Faith, and she believed and was baptized.

But not long thereafter, as she was praying in the church by the Boyne, the sky darkened and she heard a sound without like the rushing of a great wind, and mingled in it were cries and lamentations, and her own name called again and again in a multitude of voices, thin and faint as the crying of curlews upon the moor. She sprang up and gazed around, calling in return, but nothing could she see, and at last the storm of cries died away, and everything was still again around the church except the singing voice of Boyne and the humming of the garden bees.

Then Ethne sank down swooning, and the monks bore her out into the air, and it was long until her heart beat and her eyes unclosed again. In that hour she fell into a sickness from which she never recovered. In no long time she died with her head upon the breast of the holy Patrick, and she was buried in the church where she had first been received by the monk; and the church was called Killethne, or the Church of Ethne, from that day forward until now.

THE HIGH DEEDS OF FINN

CHAPTER IX

The Boyhood of Finn Mac Cumhal

In Ireland long ago, centuries before the English appeared in that country, there were kings and chiefs, lawyers and merchants, men of the sword and men of the book, men who tilled their own ground and men who tilled the ground of others, just as there are now. But there was also, as ancient poets and historians tell us, a great company or brotherhood of men who were bound to no fixed calling, unless it was to fight for the High King of Ireland whenever foes threatened him from within the kingdom or without it. This company was called the Fianna of Erinn. They were mighty hunters and warriors, and though they had great possessions in land, and rich robes, and gold ornaments, and weapons wrought with beautiful chasing and with coloured enamels, they lived mostly a free out-door life in the light hunting-booths which they made in the woods where the deer and the wolf ranged. There were then vast forests in Ireland, which are all gone now, and there were also, as there still are, many great and beautiful lakes and rivers, swarming with fish and water-fowl. In the forests and on the mountain sides roamed the wild boar and the wolf, and great herds of deer, some of giant size, whose enormous antlers are sometimes found when bogs are being drained. The Fianna chased these and the wolves with great dogs, whose courage and strength and beauty were famous throughout Europe, and which they prized and loved above all things. To the present day in Ireland there still remain some of this breed of Irish hounds, but the giant deer and the wolf are gone, and the Fianna of Erinn live only in the ancient books that were written of them, and in the tales that are still told of them in the winter evenings by the Irish peasant's fireside.

The Fianna were under the rule of one great captain or chief, and at the time I tell of his name was Cumhal, son of Trenmor. Now a tribe or family of the Fianna named the Clan Morna, or Sons of Morna, rose in rebellion against Cumhal, for they were jealous and greedy of his power and glory, and sought to have the captaincy for themselves. They defeated and slew him at the battle of Cnucha, which is now called Castleknock, near the City of the Hurdle Ford, which is the name that Dublin still bears in the Irish tongue. Goll, son of Morna, slew Cumhal, and they spoiled him of the Treasure Bag of the Fianna, which was a bag made of a crane's skin and having in it jewels of great price, and magic weapons, and strange things that had come down from far-off days when the Fairy Folk and mortal men battled for the lordship of Ireland. The Bag with its treasures was given to Lia, the chief of Luachar in Connacht, who had the keeping of it before, for he was the treasurer of Cumhal, and he was the first man who had wounded Cumhal in the battle when he fell.

Cumhal's wife was named Murna, and she bore him two sons. The elder was named Tulcha, and he fled from the country for fear of Goll and took service with the King of Scotland. The younger was born after Cumhal's death, and his name was called Demna. And because his mother feared that the sons of Morna would find him out and kill him, she gave him to a Druidess and another wise woman of Cumhal's household, and bade them take him away and rear him as best they could. So they took him into the wild woods on the Slieve Bloom Mountains, and there they trained him to hunt and fish and to throw the spear, and he grew strong, and as beautiful as a child of the Fairy Folk. If he were in the same field with a hare he could run so that the hare could never leave the field, for Demna was always before it. He could run down and slay a stag with no dogs to help him, and he could kill a wild duck on the wing with a stone from his sling. And the Druidess taught him the learning of the time, and also the story of his race and nation, and told him of his right to be captain of the Fianna of Erinn when his day of destiny should come.

One day, while still a boy, he was roaming through the woods when he came to the mansion of a great lord, where many boys, sons of the chief men of Ireland, were being trained in manly arts and exercises. He found them playing at hurling, and they invited him to join them. He did so, but the side he was on won too easily, so they divided again, and yet again, giving fewer and fewer to Demna's side, till at last he alone drove the ball to the goal through them all, flashing among them as a salmon among a shoal of minnows. And then their anger and jealousy rose and grew bitter against the stranger, and instead of honouring him as gallant lads of gentle blood should have done they fell upon him with their hurling clubs and sought to kill him. But Demna felled seven of them to the ground and put the rest to flight, and then went his way home. When the boys told what had happened the chief asked them who it was that had defeated and routed them single-handed. They said, "It was a tall shapely lad, and very fair (_finn_)." So the name of Finn, the Fair One, clung to him thenceforth, and by that name he is known to this day.

By and by Finn gathered round him a band of youths who loved him for his strength and valour and for his generous heart, and with them he went hunting in the forests. And Goll, and the sons of Morna, who were now captains of the Fianna under the High King, began to hear tales of him and his exploits, and they sent trackers to inquire about him, for they had an inkling of who this wonderful fair-haired youth might be. Finn's foster mothers heard of this. "You must leave this place," they said to him, "and see our faces no more, for if Goll's men find you here they will slay you. We have cherished the blood of Cumhal," they said, "and now our work is done. Go, and may blessing and victory go with you." So Finn departed with naught but his weapons and his hunting gear, very sorrowful at leaving the wise and loving friends who had fostered his childhood; but deep in his heart was a wild and fierce delight at the thought of the trackless ways he would travel, and the wonders he would see; and all the future looked to him as beautiful and dim as the mists that fill a mountain glen under the morning sun.

Now after the death of Cumhal, his brother Crimmal and a few others of the aged warriors of the Fianna, who had not fallen in the fight at Cnucha, fled away into Connacht, and lived there in the deepest recesses of a great forest, where they hoped the conquerors might never find them. Here they built themselves a poor dwelling of tree branches, plastered with mud and roofed with reeds from the lake, and here they lived on what game they could kill or snare in the wild wood; and harder and harder it grew, as age and feebleness crept on them, to find enough to eat, or to hew wood for their fire. In this retreat, never having seen the friendly face of man, they were one day startled to hear voices and the baying of hounds approaching them through the wood, and they thought that the sons of Morna were upon them at last, and that their hour of doom was at hand. Soon they perceived a company of youths coming towards their hut, with one in front who seemed to be their leader. Taller he was by a head than the rest, broad shouldered, and with masses of bright hair clustering round his forehead, and he carried in his hand a large bag made of some delicate skin and stained in patterns of red and blue. The old men thought when they saw him of a saying there was about the mighty Lugh, who was brother to the wife of Cumhal, that when he came among his army as they mustered for battle, men felt as though they beheld the rising of the sun. As they came near, the young men halted and looked upon the elders with pity, for their clothing of skins was ragged and the weapons they strove to hold were rusted and blunt, and except for their proud bearing and the fire in their old eyes they looked more like aged and worthless slaves in the household of a niggardly lord than men who had once been the flower of the fighting men of Erinn.

But the tall youth stepped in front of his band and cried aloud—

"Which of ye is Crimmal, son of Trenmor?" And one of the elders said, "I am Crimmal." Then tears filled the eyes of the youth, and he knelt down before the old man and put his hands in his.

"My lord and chief," he said, "I am Finn, son of Cumhal, and the day of deliverance is come."

So the youths brought in the spoils of their hunting, and yet other spoils than these; and that night there was feasting and joy in the lonely hut. And Crimmal said—

"It was foretold to us that one day the blood of Cumhal should be avenged, and the race of Cumhal should rule the Fianna again. This was the sign that the coming champion should give of his birth and destiny; he was to bear with him the Treasure Bag of Cumhal and the sacred things that were therein."

Finn said, "Ye know the Bag and its treasures, tell us if these be they." And he laid his skin bag on the knees of Crimmal.

Crimmal opened it, and he took out the jewels of sovranty the magic spear-head made by the smiths of the Fairy Folk, and he said, "These be the treasures of Cumhal; truly the ripeness of the time is come."

And Finn then told the story of how he had won these things.

"But yesterday morning," he said, "we met on our way a woman of noble aspect, and she knelt over the body of a slain youth. When she lifted her head as we drew near, tears of blood ran down her cheeks, and she cried to me, 'Whoever thou art, I bind thee by the bonds of the sacred ordinances of the Gael that thou avenge my wrong. This was my son Glonda,' she said, 'my only son, and he was slain to-day wantonly by

67

the Lord of Luachar and his men.' So we went, my company and I, to the Dún of the Lord of Luachar, and found an earthen rampart with a fosse before it, and on the top of the rampart was a fence of oaken posts interlaced with wattles, and over this we saw the many-coloured thatch of a great dwelling-house, and its white walls painted with bright colours under the broad eaves. So I stood forth and called to the Lord of Luachar and bade him make ready to pay an eric to the mother of Glonda, whatsoever she should demand. But he laughed at us and cursed us and bade us begone. Then we withdrew into the forest, but returned with a great pile of dry brushwood, and while some of us shot stones and arrows at whoever should appear above the palisade, others rushed up with bundles of brushwood and laid it against the palisade and set it on fire, and the Immortal Ones sent a blast of wind that set the brushwood and palisade quickly in a blaze, and through that fiery gap we charged in shouting. And half of the men of Luachar we killed and the rest fled, and the Lord of Luachar I slew in the doorway of his palace. We took a great spoil then, O Crimmal—these vessels of bronze and silver, and spears and bows, smoked bacon and skins of Greek wine; and in a great chest of yewwood we found this bag. All these things shall now remain with you, and my company shall also remain to hunt for you and protect you, for ye shall know want and fear no longer while ye live."

And Finn said, "I would fain know if my mother Murna still lives, or if she died by the sons of Morna."

Crimmal said, "After thy father's death, Finn, she was wedded to Gleor, Lord of Lamrigh, in the south, and she still lives in honour with him, and the sons of Morna have let her be. Didst thou never see her since she gave thee, an infant, to the wise women on the day of Cnucha?"

"I remember," said Finn, "when I was, as they tell me, but six years old, there came one day to our shieling in the woods of Slieve Bloom a chariot with bronze-shod wheels and a bronze wolf's head at the end of the pole, and two horsemen riding with it, besides him who drove. A lady was in it, with a gold frontlet on her brow and her cloak was fastened with a broad golden brooch. She came into our hut and spoke long with my foster-mothers, and me she clasped in her arms and kissed many times, and I felt her tears on my face. And they told me afterwards that this was Murna of the White Neck, and my mother. If she have suffered no harm at the hands of the sons of Morna, so much the less is the debt that they shall one day pay."

Now it is to be told what happened to Finn at the house of Finegas the Bard. Finn did not deem that the time had come for him to seize the captaincy of the Fianna until he had perfected himself in wisdom and learning. So on leaving the shelter of the old men in the wood he went to learn wisdom and the art of poetry from Finegas, who dwelt by the River Boyne, near to where is now the village of Slane. It was a belief among the poets of Ireland that the place of the revealing of poetry is always by the margin of water. But Finegas had another reason for the place where he made his dwelling, for there was an old prophecy that whoever should first eat of the Salmon of Knowledge that lived in the River Boyne, should become the wisest of men. Now this salmon was called Finntan in ancient times and was one of the Immortals, and he might be eaten and yet live. But in the time of Finegas he was called the Salmon of the Pool of Fec, which is the place where the fair river broadens out into a great still pool, with green banks softly sloping upward from the clear brown water. Seven years was Finegas watching the pool, but not until after Finn had come to be his disciple was the salmon caught. Then Finegas gave it to Finn to cook, and bade him eat none of it. But when Finegas saw him coming with the fish, he knew that something had chanced to the lad, for he had been used to have the eye of a young man but now he had the eye of a sage. Finegas said, "Hast thou eaten of the salmon?"

"Nay," said Finn, "but it burnt me as I turned it upon the spit and I put my thumb in my mouth" And Finegas smote his hands together and was silent for a while. Then he said to the lad who stood by obediently, "Take the salmon and eat it, Finn, son of Cumhal, for to thee the prophecy is come. And now go hence, for I can teach thee no more, and blessing and victory be thine."

With Finegas, Finn learned the three things that make a poet, and they are Fire of Song, and Light of Knowledge, and the Art of Extempore Recitation. Before he departed he made this lay to prove his art, and it is called "The Song of Finn in Praise of May":—

May Day! delightful day!
Bright colours play the vales along. Now wakes at morning's slender ray,
Wild and gay, the blackbird's song.

Now comes the bird of dusty hue,
The loud cuckoo, the summer-lover; Branching trees are thick with leaves;
The bitter, evil time is over.

Swift horses gather nigh
Where half dry the river goes; Tufted heather crowns the height;
Weak and white the bogdown blows.

Corncrake sings from eve till morn,
Deep in corn, a strenuous bard! Sings the virgin waterfall,
White and tall, her one sweet word.

Loaded bees of little power
Goodly flower-harvest win; Cattle roam with muddy flanks;
Busy ants go out and in.

Through, the wild harp of the wood
Making music roars the gale— Now it slumbers without motion,
On the ocean sleeps the sail.

Men grow mighty in the May,
Proud and gay the maidens grow; Fair is every wooded height;
Fair and bright the plain below.

A bright shaft has smit the streams,
With gold gleams the water-flag; Leaps the fish, and on the hills
Ardour thrills the flying stag.

Carols loud the lark on high,
Small and shy, his tireless lay, Singing in wildest, merriest mood
Of delicate-hued, delightful May.[20]

CHAPTER X

The Coming of Finn

And now we tell how Finn came to the captaincy of the Fianna of Erinn.

At this time Ireland was ruled by one of the mightiest of her native kings, Conn, son of Felimy, who was surnamed Conn of the Hundred Battles. And Conn sat in his great banqueting hall at Tara, while the yearly Assembly of the lords and princes of the Gael went forward, during which it was the inviolable law that no quarrel should be raised and no weapon drawn, so that every man who had a right to come to that Assembly might come there and sit next his deadliest foe in peace. Below him sat at meat the provincial kings and the chiefs of clans, and the High King's officers and fighting-men of the Fianna, with Goll and the sons of Morna at their head. And there, too, sat modestly a strange youth, tall and fair, whom no one had seen in that place before. Conn marked him with the eye of a king that is accustomed to mark men, and by and by he sent him a horn full of wine from his own table and bade the youth declare his name and lineage. "I am Finn, son of Cumhal," said the youth, standing among them, tall as a warriors spear, and a start and a low murmur ran through the Assembly while the captains of the Fianna stared upon him like men who see a vision of the dead. "What seek you here?" said Conn, and Finn replied, "To be your man, O King, and to do you service in war as my father did." "It is well," said the King. "Thou art a friend's son and the son of man of trust." So Finn put his hand in the Kind's and swore fealty and service to him, and Conn set him beside his own son Art, and all fell to talking again and wondering what new things that day would bring forth, and the feasting went merrily forward.

Now at this time the people of the royal burg of Tara were sorely afflicted by a goblin of the Fairy Folk, who was wont to approach the place at night-fall, there to work what harm to man, or beast, or dwelling that he found in his evil mind to do. And he could not be resisted, for as he came he played on a magic harp a strain so keen and sweet, that each man who heard it must needs stand entranced and motionless until the fairy music had passed away. The King proclaimed a mighty reward to any man who would save Tara from the goblin, and Finn thought in his heart, "I am the man to do that." So he said to the King, "Shall I have my rightful heritage as captain of the Fianna of Erin if I slay the goblin?" Conn said, "I promise thee that," and he bound himself by the sureties of all the provincial Kings of Ireland and of the Druid Kithro and his magicians.

Now there was among the following of Conn a man named Fiacha, who had been as a youth a trusty friend and follower of Cumhal. He came to Finn and brought with him a spear having a head of dark bronze with glittering edges, and fastened with thirty rivets of Arabian gold, and the spear-head was laced up within a leathern case. "By this weapon of enchantment," said Fiacha, "you shall overcome the enchanter," and he taught Finn what to do with it when the hour of need should come.

So Finn took the spear, and left the strings of the case loose, and he paced with it towards night-fall around the ramparts of royal Tara. And when he had once made the circuit of the rampart, and the light had now almost quite faded from the summer sky, and the wide low plains around the Hill of Tara were a sea of white mist, he heard far off in the deepening gloom the first notes of the fairy harp. Never such music was made by mortal hand, for it had in it sorrows that man has never felt, and joys for which man has no name, and it seemed as if a man listening to that music might burst from time into eternity and be as one of the Immortals for evermore. And Finn listened, amazed and rapt, till at last as the triumphant melody grew nearer and louder he saw dimly a Shadow Shape playing as it were on a harp, and coming swiftly towards him. Then with a mighty effort he roused himself from dreams, and tore the cover from the spear-head and laid the metal to his brow. And the demoniac energy that had been beaten into the blade by the hammers of unearthly craftsmen in ancient days thrilled through him and made him fighting-mad, and he rushed forward shouting his battle-cry, and swinging the spear aloft. But the Shadow turned and fled before him, and Finn chased it northward to the Fairy Mound of Slieve Fuad, and there he drove the spear through its back. And what it was that fell there in the night, and what it was that passed like the shadow of a shadow into the Fairy Mound, none can tell, but Finn bore back with him next day a pale, sorrowful head on the point of Fiacha's spear, and the goblin troubled the folk of royal Tara no more.

But Conn of the Hundred Battles called the Fianna together, and he set Finn at his right hand and said, "Here is your Captain by birth-right and by sword-right. Let who will now obey him hence-forward, and who will not, let him go in peace and serve Arthur of Britain or Arist of Alba, or whatsoever King he will." And Goll, son of Morna, said, "For my part I will be Finn's man under thee, O King," and he swore obedience and loyalty to Finn before them all. Nor was it hard for any man to step where Goll had gone before, so they all took their oaths of Fian service to Finn mac Cumhal. And thus it was that Finn came to the captaincy of the Fianna of Erinn, and he ruled the Fianna many a year till he died in battle with the Clan Urgrenn at Brea upon the Boyne.

CHAPTER XI

Finn's Chief Men

With the coming of Finn did the Fianna of Erinn come to their glory, and with his life their glory passed away. For he ruled them as no other captain ever did, both strongly and wisely, and never bore a grudge against any, but freely forgave a man all offences save disloyalty to his lord. Thus it is told that Conan, son of the Lord of Luachar, him who had the Treasure Bag and whom Finn slew at Rath Luachar, was for seven years an outlaw and marauder, harrying the Fians, and killing here a man and there a hound, and firing their dwellings, and raiding their cattle. At last they ran him to a corner at Cam Lewy in Munster, and when he saw that he could escape no more he stole upon Finn as he sat down after a chase, and flung his arms round him from behind, holding him fast and motionless. Finn knew who held him thus and said, "What wilt thou Conan?" Conan said, "To make a covenant of service and fealty with thee, for I may no longer evade thy wrath." So Finn laughed and said, "Be it so, Conan, and if thou prove faithful and valiant, I also will keep faith." And Conan served him for thirty years, and no man of all the Fianna was keener and hardier in fight. There was also another Conan, namely, mac Morna, who was big and bald, and unwieldy in manly exercises, but whose tongue was bitter and scurrilous; no high brave thing was done that Conan the Bald did not mock and belittle. It is said that when he was stripped he showed down his back and buttocks a black sheep's fleece instead of a man's skin, and this is the way it came about. One day when Conan and certain others of the Fianna were hunting in the forest they came to a stately Dún, white-walled, with coloured thatching on the roof, and they entered it to seek hospitality. But when they were within they found! no man, but a great empty hall with pillars of cedar wood and silken hangings about it, like the hall of a wealthy lord. In the midst there was a table set forth with a sumptuous feast of boar's flesh and venison, and a great vat of yew wood full of red wine, and cups of gold and silver. So they set themselves gaily to eat and drink, for they were hungry from the chase, and talk and laughter were loud around the board. But one of them ere long started to his feet with a cry of fear and wonder, and they all looked round, and saw before their eyes the tapestried walls changing to rough wooden balks and the ceiling to foul sooty thatch like that of a herdsman's hut. So they knew they were being entrapped by some enchantment of the Fairy Folk, and all sprang to their feet and made for the doorway, that was no longer high and stately but was shrinking to the size of a fox earth,—all but Conan the Bald, who was gluttonously devouring the good things on the table, and heeded nothing else. Then they shouted to him, and as the last of them went out he strove to rise and follow, but found himself limed to the chair so that he could not stir. So two of the Fianna, seeing his plight, rushed back and seized his arms and tugged with all their might, and if they dragged him away, they left the most part of his raiment and his skin sticking to the chair. Then, not knowing what else to do with him in his sore plight they clapped upon his back the nearest thing they could find, which was the skin of a black sheep that they took from a peasant's flock hard by, and it grew there, and Conan wore it till his death.

Though Conan was a coward and rarely adventured himself in battle with the Fianna, it is told that once a good man fell by his hand. This was on the day of the great battle with the pirate horde on the Hill of Slaughter in Kerry.[21] For Liagan, one of the invaders, stood out before the hosts and challenged the bravest of the Fians to single combat, and the Fians, in mockery, thrust Conan forth to the fight. When he appeared, Liagan laughed, for he had more strength than wit, and he said, "Silly is thy visit, thou bald old man." And as Conan still approached, Liagan lifted his hand fiercely, and Conan said, "Truly thou art in more peril from the man behind than from the man in front." Liagan looked round; and in that instant Conan swept off his head and then threw down his sword and ran for shelter to the ranks of the laughing Fians. But Finn was very wroth because he had won the victory by a trick.

And one of the chiefest of the friends of Finn was Dermot of the Love Spot. He was so fair and noble to look on that no woman could refuse him love, and it was said that he never knew weariness, but his step was as light at the end of the longest day of battle or the chase as it was at the beginning. Between him and Finn there was great love until the day when Finn, then an old man, was to wed Grania, daughter of Cormac the High King; but Grania bound Dermot by the sacred ordinances of the Fian chivalry to fly with her on her wedding night, which thing, sorely against his will, he did, and thereby got his death. But Grania went back to Finn, and when the Fianna saw her they laughed through all the camp in bitter mockery, for they would not have given one of the dead man's fingers for twenty such as Grania.

Others of the chief men that Finn had were Keelta mac Ronan, who was one of his house-stewards and a strong warrior as well as a golden-tongued reciter of tales and poems. And there was Oisín, the son of Finn, the greatest poet of the Gael, of whom more shall be told hereafter. And Oisín had a son Oscar, who was the fiercest fighter in battle among all the Fians. He slew in his maiden battle three kings, and in his fury he also slew by mischance his own friend and condisciple Linne. His wife was the fair Aideen, who died of grief after Oscar's death in the battle of Gowra, and Oisín buried her on Ben Edar (Howth), and raised over her the great cromlech which is there to this day.

Another good man that Finn had was Geena, the son of Luga; his mother was the warrior-daughter of Finn, and his father was a near kinsman of hers. He was nurtured by a woman that bore the name of Fair Mane, who had brought up many of the Fianna to manhood. When his time to take arms was come he stood before Finn and made his covenant of fealty, and Finn gave him the captaincy of a band. But mac Luga proved slothful and selfish, for ever vaunting himself and his weapon-skill and never training his men to the chase of deer or boar, and he used to beat his hounds and his serving-men. At last the Fians under him came with their whole company to Finn at Loch Lena in Killarney, and there they laid their complaint against mac Luga, and said, "Choose now, O Finn, whether you will have us, or the son of Luga by himself."

Then Finn sent to mac Luga and questioned him, but mac Luga could say nothing to the point as to why the Fianna would none of him. Then Finn taught him the things befitting a youth of noble birth and a captain of men, and they were these:—

"Son of Luga, if armed service be thy design, in a great man's household be quiet, be surly in the narrow pass."

"Without a fault of his beat not thy hound; until thou ascertain her guilt, bring not a charge against thy wife."

"In battle, meddle not with a buffoon, for, O mac Luga, he is but a fool."

"Censure not any if he be of grave repute; stand not up to take part in a brawl; have nought to do with a madman or a wicked one."

"Two-thirds of thy gentleness be shown to women and to those that creep on the floor (little children) and to poets, and be not violent to the common people."

"Utter not swaggering speech, nor say thou wilt not yield what is right; it is a shameful thing to speak too stiffly unless that it be feasible to carry out thy words."

"So long as thou shalt live, thy lord forsake not; neither for gold nor for other reward in the world abandon one whom thou art pledged to protect."

"To a chief do not abuse his people, for that is no work for a gentleman."

"Be no talebearer, nor utterer of falsehoods; be not talkative nor rashly censorious. Stir not up strife against thee, however good a man thou be."

"Be no frequenter of the drinking-house, nor given to carping at the old; meddle not with a man of mean estate."

"Dispense thy meat freely, have no niggard for thy familiar."

"Force not thyself upon a chief, nor give him cause to speak ill of thee."

"Stick to thy gear, hold fast to thy arms till the stern fight with its weapon-glitter be well ended."

"Be more apt to give than to deny, and follow after gentleness, O son of Luga."[22]

And the son of Luga, it is written, heeded these counsels and gave up his bad ways, and he became one of the best of Finn's men.

Such-like things also Finn taught to all his followers, and the best of them became like himself in valour and gentleness and generosity. Each of them loved the repute of his comrades more than his own, and each would say that for all noble qualities there was no man in the breadth of the world worthy to be thought of beside Finn.

It was said of him that "he gave away gold as if it were the leaves of the woodland, and silver as if it were the foam of the sea," and that whatever he had bestowed upon any man, if he fell out with him afterwards, he was never known to bring it against him.

Sang the poet Oisín of him once to St Patrick:—

"These are the things that were dear to Finn—
The din of battle, the banquet's glee,

The bay of his hounds through the rough glen ringing.
And the blackbird singing in Letter Lee,

"The shingle grinding along the shore
When they dragged his war-boats down to sea,
The dawn-wind whistling his spears among,
And the magic song of his minstrels three."

In the time of Finn no one was ever admitted to be one of the Fianna of Erinn unless he could pass through many severe tests of his worthiness. He must be versed in the Twelve Books of Poetry and must himself be skilled to make verse in the rime and metre of the masters of Gaelic poesy. Then he was buried to his middle in the earth, and must, with a shield and a hazel stick, there defend himself against nine warriors casting spears at him, and if he were wounded he was not accepted. Then his hair was woven into braids and he was chased through the forest by the Fians. If he were overtaken, or if a braid of his hair were disturbed, or if a dry stick cracked under his foot, he was not accepted. He must be able to leap over a lath level with his brow and to run at full speed under level with his knee, and he must be able while running to draw out a thorn from his foot and never slacken speed. He must take no dowry with a wife.

It was said that one of the Fians, namely Keelta, lived on to a great age, and saw St Patrick, by whom he was baptized into the faith of the Christ, and to whom he told many tales of Finn and his men, which Patrick's scribe wrote down. And once Patrick asked him how it was that the Fianna became so mighty and so glorious that all Ireland sang of their deeds, as Ireland has done ever since. Keelta answered, "Truth was in our hearts and strength in our arms, and what we said, that we fulfilled."

This was also told of Keelta after he had seen St Patrick and received the Faith. He chanced to be one day by Leyney in Connacht, where the Fairy Folk of the Mound of Duma were wont to be sorely harassed and spoiled every year by pirates from oversea. They called Keelta to their aid, and by his counsel and valour the invaders were overcome and driven home, but Keelta was sorely wounded. Then Keelta asked that Owen the seer of the Fairy Folk might foretell him how long he had to live, for he was already a very aged man. Owen said, "It will be seventeen years, O Keelta of fair fame, till thou fall by the pool of Tara, and grievous that will be to all the King's household." "Even so did my chief and lord, my guardian and loving Protector, Finn, foretell to me," said Keelta. "And now what fee will ye give me for my rescue of you from the worst affliction that ever befell you?" "A great reward," said the Fairy Folk, "even youth; for by our art we shall change you into young man again with all the strength and activity of your prime." "Nay, God forbid," said Keelta "that I should take upon me a shape of sorcery, or any other than that which my Maker, the true and glorious God, hath bestowed upon me." And the Fairy Folk said, "It is the word of a true warrior and hero, and the thing that thou sayest is good." So they healed his wounds, and every bodily evil that he had, and he wished them blessing and victory, and went his way.

CHAPTER XII

The Tale of Vivionn the Giantess

One day Finn and Goll, Keelta and Oscar, and others of the Fianna, were resting after the hunt on a certain hill now called the Ridge of the Dead Woman, and their meal was being got ready, when a girl of the kin of the giants came striding up and sat down among them. "Didst thou ever see a woman so tall?"

asked Finn of Goll. "By my troth," said Goll, "never have I or any other seen a woman so big." She took her hand out of her bosom and on her long slender fingers there were three gold rings each as thick as an ox's yoke. "Let us question her," said Goll, and Finn said, "If we stood up, perchance she might hear us."

So they all rose to their feet, but the giantess, on that, rose up too. "Maiden," said Finn, "if thou have aught to say to us or to hear from us, sit down and lean thine elbow on the hill-side." So she lay down and Finn bade her say whence she came and what was her will with them. "Out of the World Oversea where the sun sets am I come," she said, "to seek thy protection, O mighty Finn." "And what is thy name?" "My name is Vivionn of the Fair Hair, and my father Treon is called King of the Land of Lasses, for he has but three sons and nine and seven score daughters, and near him is a King who hath one daughter and eight score sons. To one of these, Æda, was I given in marriage sorely against my will. Three times now have I fled from him. And this time it was fishermen whom the wind blew to us from off this land who told us of a mighty lord here, named Finn, son of Cumhal, who would let none be wronged or oppressed, but he would be their friend and champion. And if thou be he, to thee am I come." Then she laid her hand in Finn's, and he bade her do the same with Goll mac Morna, who was second in the Fian leadership, and she did so.

Then the maiden took from her head a jewelled golden helmet, and immediately her hair flowed out in seven score tresses, fair, curly and golden, at the abundance of which all stood amazed; and Finn said, "By the Immortals that we adore, but King Cormac and the poetess Ethne and the fair women-folk of the Fianna would deem it a marvel to see this girl. Tell us now, maiden, what portion wilt thou have of meat and drink? will that of a hundred of us suffice thee?" The girl then saw Cnu, the dwarf harper of Finn, who had just been playing to them, and she said, "Whatever thou givest to yon little man that bears the harp, be it much or little, the same, O Finn, will suffice for me."

Then she begged a drink from them, and Finn called his gillie, Saltran, and bade him fetch the full of a certain great goblet with water from the ford; now this goblet was of wood, and it held as much as nine of the Fianna could drink. The maiden poured some of the water into her right hand and drank three sips of it, and scattered the rest over the Fianna, and she and they burst out laughing. Finn said, "On thy conscience, girl, what ailed thee not to drink out of the goblet?" "Never," she replied, "have I drunk out of any vessel but there was a rim of gold to it, or at least of silver."

And now Keelta looking up perceived a tall youth coming swiftly towards them, who, when he approached, seemed even bigger than was the maiden. He wore a rough hairy cape over his shoulder and beneath that a green cloak fastened by a golden brooch; his tunic was of royal satin, and he bore a red shield slung over his shoulders, and a spear with a shaft as thick as a man's leg was in his hand; a gold-hilted sword hung by his side. And his face, which was smooth-shaven, was comelier than that of any of the sons of men.

When he came near, seeing among the Fians a stir of alarm at this apparition, Finn said, "Keep every one of you his place, let neither warrior nor gillie address him. Know any of you this champion?" "I know him," said the maiden; "that is even he to escape from whom I am come to thee, O Finn." And she sat down between Finn and Goll. But the stranger drew near, and spake never a word, but before any one could tell what he would be at he thrust fiercely and suddenly with his spear at the girl, and the shaft stood out a hand's breadth at her back. And she fell gasping, but the young man drew his weapon out and passed rapidly through the crowd and away.

Then Finn cried, red with wrath, "Ye have seen! Avenge this wicked deed, or none of you aspire to Fianship again." And the whole company sprang to their feet and gave chase to that murderer, save only Finn and Goll, who stayed by the dying maiden. And they ran him by hill and plain to the great Bay of

75

Tralee and down to the Tribute Point, where the traders from oversea were wont to pay their dues, and there he set his face to the West and took the water. By this time four of the Fianna had outstripped the rest, namely, Keelta, and Dermot, and Glas, and Oscar, son of Oisín. Of these Keelta was first, and just as the giant was mid-leg in the waves he hurled his spear and it severed the thong of the giant's shield so that it fell off in the water. And as the giant paused, Keelta seized his spear and tore it from him. But the giant waded on, and soon the Fians were floundering in deep water while the huge form, thigh deep, was seen striding towards the setting sun. And a great ship seemed to draw near, and it received him, and then departed into the light, but the Fians returned in the grey evening, bearing the spear and the great shield to Finn. There they found the maiden at point of death, and they laid the weapons before her. "Goodly indeed are these arms," she said, "for that is the Thunder Spear of the King Oversea and the shield is the Red Branch Shield," for it was covered with red arabesques. Then she bestowed her bracelets on Finn's three harpers, the dwarf Cnu, and Blanit his wife, and the harper Daira. And she bade Finn care for her burial, that it should be done becomingly, "for under thy honour and protection I got my death, and it was to thee I came into Ireland." So they buried her and lamented her, and made a great far-seen mound over her grave, which is called the Ridge of the Dead Woman, and set up a pillar stone upon it with her name and lineage carved in Ogham-crave.[23]

CHAPTER XIII

The Chase of the Gilla Dacar

In the reign of Cormac mac Art, grandson of Conn of the Hundred Battles, the order of precedence and dignity in the court of the High King at Tara was as follows: First came great Cormac, the kingly, the hospitable, warrior and poet, and he was supreme over all. Next in order came the five kings of the five Provinces of Ireland, namely, Ulster, Munster, Connacht, Leinster, and Mid-Erinn. After these ranked the captains of the royal host, of whom Finn, son of Cumhal, was the chief.

Now the privileges of the Fianna of Erinn were many and great; to wit, in every county in Ireland one townland, and in every townland a cartron of land, and in the house of every gentleman the right to have a young deer-hound or a beagle kept at nurse from November to May, together with many other taxes and royalties not to be recounted here. But if they had these many and great privileges, yet greater than these were the toils and hardships which they had to endure, in guarding the coasts of all Ireland from oversea invaders and marauders, and in keeping down all robbers and outlaws and evil folk within the kingdom, for this was the duty laid upon them by their bond of service to the King.

Now the summer half of the year was wont to be ended by a great hunting in one of the forests of Ireland, and so it was that one All-hallowtide, when the great banquet of Finn in his Dún on the Hill of Allen was going forward, and the hall resounded with cheerful talk and laughter and with the music of tympan and of harp, Finn asked of the assembled captains in what part of Erinn they should proceed to beat up game on the morrow. And it was agreed among them to repair to the territory of Thomond and Desmond in Munster; and from Allen they set out accordingly and came to the Hill of Knockany. Thence they threw out the hunt and sent their bands of beaters through many a gloomy ravine and by many a rugged hill-pass and many a fair open plain. Desmond's high hills, called now Slievelogher, they beat, and the smooth, swelling hills of Slievenamuck, and the green slopes of grassy Slievenamon, and the towering rough crags of the Decies, and thence on to the dark woods of Belachgowran.

While the great hunt was going forward Finn with certain of his chief captains sat on a high mound to overlook it. There, with Finn, were Goll and Art mac Morna, and Liagan the swift runner, and Dermot of the Love Spot, and Keelta, son of Ronan, and there also was Conan the Bald, the man of scurrilous tongue, and a score or so more. Sweet it was to Finn and his companions to hear from the woods and wildernesses around them the many-tongued baying of the hounds and the cries and whistling of the beaters, the shouting of the strong men and the notes of the Fian hunting-horn.

When they had sat there awhile one of Finn's men came running quickly towards him and said—

"A stranger is approaching us from the westward, O Finn, and I much mislike his aspect."

With that all the Fians looked up and beheld upon the hillside a huge man, looking like some Fomorian marauder, black-visaged and ugly, with a sour countenance and ungainly limbs. On his back hung a dingy black shield, on his misshapen left thigh he wore a sharp broad-bladed sword; projecting over his shoulder were two long lances with broad rusty heads. He wore garments that looked as if they had been buried in a cinder heap, and a loose ragged mantle. Behind him there shambled a sulky, ill-shapen mare with a bony carcase and bowed knees, and on her neck a clumsy iron halter. With a rope her master hauled her along, with violent jerks that seemed as if they would wrench her head from her scraggy neck, and ever and anon the mare would stand and jib, when the man laid on her ribs such blows from a strong ironshod cudgel that they sounded like the surges of the sea beating on a rocky coast. Short as was the distance from where the man and his horse were first perceived to where Finn was standing, it was long ere they traversed it. At last, however, he came into the presence of Finn and louted before him, doing obeisance. Finn lifted his hand over him and bade him speak, and declare his business and his name and rank. "I know not," said the fellow, "of what blood I am, gentle or simple, but only this, that I am a wight from oversea looking for service and wages. And as I have heard of thee, O Finn, that thou art not wont to refuse any man, I came to take service with thee if thou wilt have me."

"Neither shall I refuse thee," said Finn; "but what brings thee here with a horse and no horseboy?"

"Good enough reason," said the stranger. "I have much ado to get meat for my own belly, seeing that I eat for a hundred men; and I will not have any horseboy meddling with my ration."

"And what name dost thou bear?"

"I am called the Gilla Dacar (the Hard Gillie)," replied he.

"Why was that name given thee?" asked Finn.

"Good enough reason for that also," spake the stranger, "for of all the lads in the world there is none harder than I am for a lord to get any service and obedience from." Then turning to Conan the Bald he said, "Whether among the Fianna is a horseman's pay or a footman's the highest?"

"A horseman's surely," said Conan, "seeing that he gets twice the pay of a footman."

"Then I am a horseman in thy service, Finn," said the gillie. "I call thee to observe that I have here a horse, and moreover that as a horseman I came among the Fianna. Have I thy authority," he went on, "to turn out my steed among thine?"

"Turn her out," quoth Finn.

Then the big man flung his mare the rope and immediately she galloped off to where the Fian horses were grazing. Here she fell to biting and kicking them, knocking out the eye of one and snapping off another's ear and breaking the leg of another with a kick.

"Take away thy mare, big man," cried Conan then, "or by Heaven and Earth were it not that Finn told thee to let her loose I would let loose her brains. Many a bad bargain has Finn made but never a worse than thou."

"By Heaven and Earth," said the gillie, "that I never will, for I have no horseboy, and I will do no horseboy's work."

Then Conan mac Morna took the iron halter and laid it on the stranger's horse and brought the beast back to Finn and held it there.

Said Finn to Conan, "I have never seen thee do horseboy's service even to far better men than this gillie. How now if thou wert to leap on the brute's back and gallop her to death over hill and dale in payment for the mischief she hath wrought among our steeds?"

At this word Conan clambered up on the back of the big man's mare, and with all his might he smote his two heels into her, but the mare never stirred.

"I perceive what ails her," said Finn. "She will never stir till she has a weight of men on her equal to that of her own rider."

Then thirteen men of the Fianna scrambled up laughing behind Conan, and the mare lay down under them, and then got up again, they still clinging to her. At this the big man said,

"It appears that you are making a sport and mockery of my mare, and that even I myself do not escape from it. It is well for me that I have not spent the rest of the year in your company, seeing what a jest ye have made of me the very first day; and I perceive, O Finn, that thou art very unlike the report that is made of thee. And now I bid thee farewell, for of thy service I have had enough."

So with downcast head and despondent looks the big gillie shambled slowly away until he had passed out of view of the Fianna, behind the shoulder of the hill. Having arrived here he tucked up his coat to his waist, and fast though be the flight of the swallow, and fast that of the roe-deer, and fast the rush of a roaring wind over a mountain top in mid-March, no faster are these than the bounding speed and furious flight of the big man down the hillside toward the West.

No sooner did the mare see that her master had departed than she too dashed uncontrollably forward and flew down the hillside after him. And as the Fians saw Conan the Bald and his thirteen companions thus carried off, willy nilly, they broke into a roar of laughter and ran alongside mocking them. But Conan, seeing that they were being carried off in the wake of the big man of evil aspect, of whom none knew whence or who he was, he was terrified and began reviling and cursing, and shouted to Finn, "A palsy seize thee, Finn; may some rascally churl, that is if possible of worse blood than thyself, have thy head, unless thou follow and rescue us wheresoever this monster shall bring us." So Finn and the Fianna ran, and the mare ran, over bare hills and by deep glens, till at last they came to Corcaguiny in Kerry, where the gillie set his face to the blue ocean, and the mare dashed in after him. But ere he did so, Liagan the Swift got two hands on the tail of the mare, though further he could not win, and he was towed in, still clinging to his hold, and over the rolling billows away they went, the fourteen Fians on the wild mare's back, and Liagan haled along by her tail.

"What is to be done now?" said Oisín to Finn when they had arrived at the beach.

"Our men are to be rescued," said Finn, "for to that we are bound by the honour of the Fianna. Whithersoever they are gone, thither must we follow and win them back by fair means or foul; but to that end we must first fit out a galley."

So in the end it was agreed that Finn and fourteen men of his bravest and best champions should sail oversea in search of the Gilla Dacar and his captives, while Oisín remained in Erinn and exercised rule over the Fianna in the place of his father. After a while, then, a swift galley was made ready by Finn and stored with victual, and with arms, and also with gold and raiment to make gifts withal if need should be. And into the ship came the fifteen valiant men, and gripped their oars, while Finn steered; and soon the sea whitened around their oarblades, and over the restless, rolling masses of the many-hued and voiceful billows, the ship clove her way to the West. And the Fians, who were wont to be wakened by the twittering of birds over their hunting booths in the greenwood, now delighted to hear, day after day as they roused themselves at morn, the lapping of the wide waters of the world against their vessel's bows, or the thunder of pounding surges when the wind blew hard.

At length after many days the sharpest-eyed of the men of Finn saw far-off what seemed a mountain rising from the sea, and to it they shaped their course. When they had come to that land they found themselves under the shadow of a great grey cliff, and beneath it slippery rocks covered with seaweed. Then Dermot, who was the most active of the company, was bidden to mount the cliff and to procure means of drawing up the rest of the party, but of what land might lie on the top of that wall of rock none of them could discover anything. Dermot, descending from the ship, then climbed with difficulty up the face of the cliff, while the others made fast their ship among the rocks. But Dermot having arrived at the top saw no habitation of man, and could compass no way of helping his companions to mount. He went therefore boldly forward into the unknown land, hoping to obtain some help, if any friendly and hospitable folk could there be found.

Before he had gone far he came into a wild wood, thick and tangled, and full of the noise of streams, and the sough of winds, and twittering of birds, and hum of bees. After he had traversed this wilderness for a while he came to a mighty tree with densely interwoven branches, and beneath it a pile of rocks, having on its summit a pointed drinking horn wreathed with rich ornament, and at its foot a well of pure bright water. Dermot, being now thirsty, took the horn and would have filled it at the well, but as he stooped down to do so he heard a loud, threatening murmur which seemed to rise from it. "I perceive," he said to himself, "that I am forbidden to drink from this well" Nevertheless thirst compelled him, and he drank his fill.

In no long time thereafter he saw an armed warrior of hostile aspect coming towards him through the wood. No courteous greeting did he give to Dermot, but began to revile him for roaming in his wood and wilderness, and for drinking his water. Thereupon they fought, and for the rest of the afternoon they took and gave hard blows neither subduing the other, till at last as darkness began to fall the warrior suddenly dived into the well and was seen no more. Dermot, vexed at this ending of the combat, then made him ready to spend the night in that place, but first he slew a deer in the wood, and made a fire, whereat he roasted pieces of the deer's flesh on spits of white hazel, and drank abundantly of the well-water, and then slept soundly through the night.

Next morning when he awakened and went to the well he found the Champion of the Well standing there and awaiting him. "It is not enough, Dermot," said he angrily, "for thee to traverse my woods at will and to drink my water, but thou must even also slay my deer." Then they closed in combat again, and dealt each other blow for blow and wound for wound till evening parted them, and the champion dived into the well as before.

On the third day it went even so; but as evening came on Dermot, watching closely, rushed at the champion just as he was about to plunge into the well, and gripped him in his arms. But none the less the Champion of the Well made his dive, and took down Dermot with him. And a darkness and faintness came over Dermot, but when he awoke, he found himself in a wide, open country, flowery and fair, and before him the walls and towers of a royal city. Thither the champion, sorely wounded, was now borne off, while a crowd of his people came round Dermot, and beat and wounded him, leaving him on the ground for dead.

After night had fallen, when all the people of the city in the Land Undersea had departed, a stalwart champion, well-armed and of bold appearance, came upon Dermot and stirred him with his foot. Dermot thereon awoke from his swoon and, warrior-like, reached out his hand for his arms. But the champion said, "Wait awhile, my son, I have not come to do thee hurt or harm. Thou hast chosen an ill place to rest and slumber in, before the city of thine enemy. Rise and follow me, and I shall bestow thee far better than that." Dermot then rose and followed the champion, and long and far they journeyed until they came to a high-towered fortress, wherein were thrice fifty valiant men-at-arms and fair women; and the daughter of that champion, a white-toothed, rosy-cheeked, smooth-handed, and black-eyebrowed maid, received Dermot, kindly and welcomefully, and applied healing herbs to his wounds, and in no long time he was made as good a man as ever. And thus he remained, and was entertained most royally with the best of viands and of liquors. The first part of every night those in that Dún were wont to spend in feasting, and the second in recreation and entertainment of the mind, with music and with poetry and bardic tales, and the third part in sound and healthful slumber, till the sun in his fiery journey rose over the heavy-clodded earth on the morrow morn.

And the King of that country, who was the champion that had aroused Dermot, told him this was the land of Sorca, and that he had showed this kindness to Dermot for that he himself had once been on wage and service with Finn, son of Cumhal "and a better master," said he, "man never had."

Now the story turns to tell of what befell Finn and the remainder of his companions when Dermot left them in the ship. After a while, seeing that he did not return, and being assured that some mischief or hindrance must have befallen him, they made an attempt to climb the cliff after him, having noted which way he went. With much toil and peril they accomplished this, and then journeying forward and following on Dermot's track, they came at last to the well in the wild wood, and saw near by the remains of the deer, and the ashes of the fire that Dermot had kindled to cook it. But from this place they could discover no track of his going. While they were debating on what should next be done, they saw riding towards them a tall warrior on a dark grey horse with a golden bridle, who greeted them courteously. From him they enquired as to whether he had seen aught of their companion, Dermot, in the wilderness. "Follow me," said the warrior, "and you shall shortly have tidings of him."

Then they followed the strange horseman into the forest by many dark and winding ways, until at last they came into a rocky ravine, where they found the mouth of a great cavern opening into the hillside. Into this they went, and the way led them downward until it seemed as if they were going into the bowels of the earth, until at last the light began to shine round them, and they came out into a lovely land of flowery plains and green woods and singing streams. In no long time thereafter they came to a great royal Dún, where he who led them was hailed as king and lord, and here, to their joy, they found their comrade, Dermot of the Love Spot, who told them of all his adventures and heard from them of theirs. This ended, and when they had been entertained and refreshed, the lord of that place spoke to Finn and said:—

"I have now, O Finn, within my fortress the fifteen stoutest heroes that the world holds. To this end have I brought you here, that ye might make war with me upon mine enemy the Champion of the Well, who is king of the land bordering on mine, and who ceases not to persecute and to harry my people because, in his arrogance, he would have all the Under World country subject to himself alone. Say now if ye will embrace this enterprise and help me to defend my own: and if not I shall set you again upon the land of Erinn."

Finn said, "What of my fifteen men that were carried away on the wild mare's back oversea?" "They are guarding the marches of my kingdom," said the King of Sorca, "and all is well with them and shall be well."

Then Finn agreed to take service with the King of Sorca, and next day they arrayed themselves for fight and went out at the head of the host. Ere long they came upon the army of the King of the Well, and with him was the King of the Greeks and a band of fierce mercenaries, and also the daughter of the Greek King, by name Tasha of the White Side, a maiden who in beauty and grace surpassed all other women of the world, as the Shannon surpasses all rivers of Erinn and the eagle surpasses all birds of the air. Now the stories of Finn and his generosity and great deeds had reached her since she was a child, and she had set her love on him, though she had never seen his face till now.

When the hosts were met, the King of the Greeks said, "Who of my men will stand forth and challenge the best of these men of Erinn to single combat that their metal may be proved, for to us it is unknown what manner of men they be." The son of the King of the Greeks said, "I will go."

So on the side of Finn, Oscar, son of Oisín, was chosen to match the son of the Greek King, and the two hosts sat down peacefully together to watch the weapon-play. And Tasha the princess sat by Finn, son of Cumhal.

Then Oscar and the King's son stepped into their fighting place, and fierce was the combat that arose between them, as when two roaring surges of the sea dash against each other in a fissure of the rocks, and the spray-cloud bursts from them high into the air. Long they fought, and many red wounds did each of them give and receive, till at last Oscar beat the Greek prince to the earth and smote off his head. Then one host groaned for woe and discouragement, while the other shouted for joy of victory, and so they parted for the night, each to their own camp.

And in the camp of the folk of Sorca they found Conan the Bald and the fourteen men that had gone with him on the mare's back.

But when night had fallen, Tasha stole from the wizard of the Greek King his branch of silver bells that when shaken would lay asleep a host of men, and with the aid of this she passed from the camp of the Greeks, and through the sentinels, and came to the tent of Finn.

On the morrow morn the King of the Greeks found that his daughter had fled to be the wife of Finn, son of Cumhal, and he offered a mighty reward to whosoever would slay Finn and bring Tasha back. But when the two armies closed in combat the Fians and the host of the King of Sorca charged so fiercely home, that they drove their foes before them as a winter gale drives before it a cloud of madly whirling leaves, and those that were not slain in the fight and the pursuit went to their own lands and abode there in peace; and thus was the war ended of the King of Sorca and the Lord of the Well.

Then the King of Sorca had Finn and his comrades before him and gave them praise and thanks for their valour. "And what reward," he said, "will ye that I make you for the saving of the kingdom of Sorca?"

"Thou wert in my service awhile," said Finn, "and I mind not that I paid thee any wage for it. Let that service even go against this, and so we are quits."

"Nay, then," cried Conan the Bald, "but what shall I have for my ride on the mare of the Gilla Dacar?"

"What wilt thou have?" said the King of Sorca.

"This," said Conan, "and nothing else will I accept. Let fourteen of the fairest women of the land of Sorca be put on that same mare, and thy wife, O King, clinging to its tail, and let them be thus haled across the sea until they come to Corcaguiny in the land of Erinn. I will have none of thy gold and silver, but the indignity that has been put upon me doth demand an honourable satisfaction."

Then the King of Sorca smiled, and he said, "Behold thy men, Finn."

Finn turned his head to look round, and as he did so the plain and the encampment of the Fairy Host vanished from his sight, and he saw himself standing on the shingly strand of a little bay, with rocky heights to right and left, crowned with yellow whin bushes whose perfume mingled with the salt sea wind. It was the spot where he had seen the Gilla Dacar and his mare take water on the coast of Kerry. Finn stared over the sea, to discover, if he might, by what means he had come thither, but nothing could he see there save the sunlit water, and nothing hear but what seemed a low laughter from the twinkling ripples that broke at his feet. Then he looked for his men, who stood there, dazed like himself and rubbing their eyes; and there too stood the Princess Tasha, who stretched out her white arms to him. Finn went over and took her hands. "Shoulder your spears, good lads!" he called to his men. "Follow me now to the Hill of Allen, and to the wedding feast of Tasha and of Finn mac Cumhal."

CHAPTER XIV

The Birth of Oisín

One day as Finn and his companions and dogs were returning from the chase to their Dún on the Hill of Allen, a beautiful fawn started up on their path and the chase swept after her, she taking the way which led to their home. Soon, all the pursuers were left far behind save only Finn himself and his two hounds Bran and Sceolaun. Now these hounds were of strange breed, for Tyren, sister to Murna, the mother of Finn, had been changed into a hound by the enchantment of a woman of the Fairy Folk, who loved Tyren's husband Ullan; and the two hounds of Finn were the children of Tyren, born to her in that shape. Of all hounds in Ireland they were the best, and Finn loved them much, so that it was said he wept but twice in his life, and once was for the death of Bran.

At last, as the chase went on down a valley side, Finn saw the fawn stop and lie down, while the two hounds began to play round her and to lick her face and limbs. So he gave commandment that none should hurt her, and she followed them to the Dún of Allen, playing with the hounds as she went.

The same night Finn awoke and saw standing by his bed the fairest woman his eyes had ever beheld.

"I am Saba, O Finn," she said, "and I was the fawn ye chased to-day. Because I would not give my love to the Druid of the Fairy Folk, who is named the Dark, he put that shape upon me by his sorceries, and I have borne it these three years. But a slave of his, pitying me, once revealed to me that if I could win to thy great Dún of Allen, O Finn, I should be safe from all enchantments and my natural shape would come to me again. But I feared to be torn in pieces by thy dogs, or wounded by thy hunters, till at last I let

82

myself be overtaken by thee alone and by Bran and Sceolaun, who have the nature of man and would do me no hurt." "Have no fear, maiden," said Finn, "we the Fianna, are free and our guest-friends are free; there is none who shall put compulsion on you here."

So Saba dwelt with Finn, and he made her his wife; and so deep was his love for her that neither the battle nor the chase had any delight for him, and for months he never left her side. She also loved him as deeply, and their joy in each other was like that of the Immortals in the Land of Youth. But at last word came to Finn that the warships of the Northmen were in the bay of Dublin, and he summoned his heroes to the fight, "for," said he to Saba, "the men of Erinn give us tribute and hospitality to defend them from the foreigner, and it were shame to take it from them and not to give that to which we, on our side, are pledged." And he called to mind that great saying of Goll mac Morna when they were once sore bested by a mighty host—"a man," said Goll, "lives after his life but not after his honour."

Seven days was Finn absent, and he drove the Northmen from the shores of Erinn. But on the eighth day he returned, and when he entered his Dún he saw trouble in the eyes of his men and of their fair womenfolk, and Saba was not on the rampart expecting his return. So he bade them tell him what had chanced, and they said—

"Whilst thou, our father and lord, wert afar off smiting the foreigner, and Saba looking ever down the pass for thy return, we saw one day as it were the likeness of thee approaching, and Bran and Sceolaun at thy heels. And we seemed also to hear the notes of the Fian hunting call blown on the wind. Then Saba hastened to the great gate, and we could not stay her, so eager was she to rush to the phantom. But when she came near, she halted and gave a loud and bitter cry, and the shape of thee smote her with a hazel wand, and lo, there was no woman there any more, but a deer. Then those hounds chased it, and ever as it strove to reach again the gate of the Dún they turned it back. We all now seized what arms we could and ran out to drive away the enchanter, but when we reached the place there was nothing to be seen, only still we heard the rushing of flying feet and the baying of dogs, and one thought it came from here, and another from there, till at last the uproar died away and all was still. What we could do, O Finn, we did; Saba is gone."

Finn then struck his hand on his breast but spoke no word, and he went to his own chamber. No man saw him for the rest of that day, nor for the day after. Then he came forth, and ordered the matters of the Fianna as of old, but for seven years thereafter he went searching for Saba through every remote glen and dark forest and cavern of Ireland, and he would take no hounds with him save Bran and Sceolaun. But at last he renounced all hope of finding her again, and went hunting as of old. One day as he was following the chase on Ben Gulban in Sligo, he heard the musical bay of the dogs change of a sudden to a fierce growling and yelping as though they were in combat with some beast, and running hastily up he and his men beheld, under a great tree, a naked boy with long hair, and around him the hounds struggling to seize him, but Bran and Sceolaun fighting with them and keeping them off. And the lad was tall and shapely, and as the heroes gathered round he gazed undauntedly on them, never heeding the rout of dogs at his feet. The Fians beat off the dogs and brought the lad home with them, and Finn was very silent and continually searched the lad's countenance with his eyes. In time, the use of speech came to him, and the story that he told was this:—

He had known no father, and no mother save a gentle hind with whom he lived in a most green and pleasant valley shut in on every side by towering cliffs that could not be scaled, or by deep chasms in the earth. In the summer he lived on fruits and such-like, and in the winter, store of provisions was laid for him in a cave. And there came to them sometimes a tall dark-visaged man, who spoke to his mother, now tenderly, and now in loud menace, but she always shrunk away in fear, and the man departed in anger. At last there came a day when the Dark Man spoke very long with his mother in all tones of entreaty and of tenderness and of rage, but she would still keep aloof and give no sign save of fear and abhorrence. Then at length the Dark Man drew near and smote her with a hazel wand; and with that he turned and went his way, but she, this time, followed him, still looking back at her son and piteously complaining. And he, when he strove to follow, found himself unable to move a limb; and crying out with rage and desolation he fell to the earth and his senses left him. When he came to himself he was on the mountain side, on Ben Gulban, where he remained some days, searching for that green and hidden valley, which he never found again. And after a while the dogs found him; but of the hind his mother and of the Dark Druid, there is no man knows the end.

Finn called his name Oisín, and he became a warrior of fame, but far more famous for the songs and tales that he made; so that of all things to this day that are told of the Fianna of Erinn, men are wont to say, "So sang the bard, Oisín, son of Finn."

CHAPTER XV

Oisín in the Land of Youth

It happened that on a misty summer morning as Finn and Oisín with many companions were hunting on the shores of Loch Lena they saw coming towards them a maiden, beautiful exceedingly, riding on a snow-white steed. She wore the garb of a queen; a crown of gold was on her head, and a dark brown mantle of silk, set with stars of red gold, fell around her and trailed on the ground. Silver shoes were on her horse's hoofs, and a crest of gold nodded on his head. When she came near she said to Finn, "From very far away I have come, and now at last I have found thee, Finn, son of Cumhal."

Then Finn said, "What is thy land and race, maiden, and what dost thou seek from me?"

"My name," she said, "is Niam of the Golden Hair. I am the daughter of the King of the Land of Youth, and that which has brought me here is the love of thy son Oisín." Then she turned to Oisín and she spoke to him in the voice of one who has never asked anything but it was granted to her, "Wilt thou go with me, Oisín, to my father's land?"

And Oisín said, "That will I, and to the world's end"; for the fairy spell had so wrought upon his heart that he cared no more for any earthly thing but to have the love of Niam of the Head of Gold.

Then the maiden spoke of the Land Oversea to which she had summoned her lover, and as she spoke a dreamy stillness fell on all things, nor did a horse shake his bit nor a hound bay, nor the least breath of wind stir in the forest trees till she had made an end. And what she said seemed sweeter and more wonderful as she spoke it than anything they could afterwards remember to have heard, but so far as they could remember it, it was this:—

"Delightful is the land beyond all dreams,
Fairer than aught thine eyes have ever seen.
There all the year the fruit is on the tree,
And all the year the bloom is on the flower.

"There with wild honey drip the forest trees;
The stores of wine and mead shall never fail.

Nor pain nor sickness knows the dweller there,
Death and decay come near him never more.

"The feast shall cloy not, nor the chase shall tire,
Nor music cease for ever through the hall;
The gold and jewels of the Land of Youth
Outshine all splendours ever dreamed by man.

"Thou shalt have horses of the fairy breed,
Thou shalt have hounds that can outrun the wind;
A hundred chiefs shall follow thee in war,
A hundred maidens sing thee to thy sleep.

"A crown of sovranty thy brow shall wear,
And by thy side a magic blade shall hang.
Thou shalt be lord of all the Land of Youth,
And lord of Niam of the Head of Gold."

As the magic song ended, the Fians beheld Oisín mount the fairy steed and hold the maiden in his arms, and ere they could stir or speak she turned her horse's head and shook the ringing bridle and down the forest glade they fled, as a beam of light flies over the land when clouds drive across the sun; and never did the Fianna behold Oisín, son of Finn, on earth again.

Yet what befell him afterwards is known. As his birth was strange so was his end, for he saw the wonders of the Land of Youth with mortal eyes and lived to tell them with mortal lips.

When the white horse with its riders reached the sea it ran lightly over the waves and soon the green woods and headlands of Erinn faded out of sight. And now the sun shone fiercely down, and the riders passed into a golden haze in which Oisín lost all knowledge of where he was or if sea or dry land were beneath his horse's hoofs. But strange sights sometimes appeared to them in the mist, for towers and palace gateways loomed up and disappeared, and once a hornless doe bounded by them chased by a white hound with one red ear, and again they saw a young maid ride by on a brown steed, bearing a golden apple in her hand, and close behind her followed a young horseman on a white steed, a purple cloak floating at his back and a gold-hilted sword in his hand. And Oisín would have asked the princess who and what these apparitions were, but Niam bade him ask nothing nor seem to notice any phantom they might see until they were come to the Land of Youth.

At last the sky gloomed above them, and Niam urged their steed faster. The wind lashed them with pelting rain, thunder roared across the sea and lightning blazed, but they held on their way till at length they came once more into a region of calm and sunshine. And now Oisín saw before him a shore of yellow sand, lapped by the ripples of a summer sea. Inland, there rose before his eye wooded hills amid which he could discern the roofs and towers of a noble city. The white horse bore them swiftly to the shore and Oisín and the maiden lighted down. And Oisín marvelled at everything around him, for never was water so blue or trees so stately as those he saw, and the forest was alive with the hum of bees and the song of birds, and the creatures that are wild in other lands, the deer and the red squirrel and the wood-dove, came, without fear, to be caressed. Soon, as they went forward, the walls of a city came in sight, and folk began to meet them on the road, some riding, some afoot, all of whom were either youths or maidens, all looking as joyous as if the morning of happy life had just begun for them, and no old or feeble person was to be seen. Niam led her companion through a towered gateway built of white and red marble, and there they were met by a glittering company of a hundred riders on black steeds and a hundred on white, and Oisín mounted a black horse and Niam her white, and they rode up to a stately palace where the King of the Land of Youth had his dwelling. And there he received them, saying in a loud voice that all the folk could hear, "Welcome, Oisín, son of Finn. Thou art come to the Land of Youth, where sorrow and weariness and death shall never touch thee. This thou hast won by thy faithfulness and valour and by the songs that thou hast made for the men of Erinn, whereof the fame is come to us, for we have here indeed all things that are delightful and joyous, but poesy alone we had not. But now we have the chief poet of the race of men to live with us, immortal among immortals, and the fair and cloudless life that we lead here shall be praised in verses as fair; even as thou, Oisín, did'st praise and adorn the short and toilsome and chequered life that men live in the world thou hast left forever. And Niam my daughter shall be thy bride, and thou shalt be in all things even as myself in the Land of Youth."

Then the heart of Oisín was filled with glory and joy, and he turned to Niam and saw her eyes burn with love as she gazed upon him. And they were wedded the same day, and the joy they had in each other grew sweeter and deeper with every day that passed. All that Niam had promised in her magic song in the wild wood when first they met, seemed faint beside the splendour and beauty of the life in the Land of Youth. In the great palace they trod on silken carpets and ate off plates of gold; the marble walls and doorways were wrought with carved work, or hung with tapestries, where forest glades, and still lakes, and flying deer were done in colours of unfading glow. Sunshine bathed that palace always, and cool winds wandered through its dim corridors, and in its courts there played fountains of bright water set about with flowers. When Oisín wished to ride, a steed of fiery but gentle temper bore him wherever he would through the pleasant land; when he longed to hear music, there came upon his thought, as though borne on the wind, crystal notes such as no hand ever struck from the strings of any harp on earth.

But Oisín's hand now never touched the harp, and the desire of singing and of making poetry never waked in him, for no one thing seemed so much better than the rest, where all perfection bloomed and glowed around him, as to make him long to praise it and to set it apart.

When seven days had passed, he said to Niam, "I would fain go a-hunting." Niam said, "So be it, dear love; to-morrow we shall take order for that." Oisín lay long awake that night, thinking of the sound of Finn's hunting-horn, and of the smell of green boughs when they kindled them to roast the deer-flesh in Fian ovens in the wildwood.

So next day Oisín and Niam fared forth on horseback, with their company of knights and maidens, and dogs leaping and barking with eagerness for the chase. Anon they came to the forest, and the hunters with the hounds made a wide circuit on this side and on that, till at last the loud clamour of the hounds told that a stag was on foot, and Oisín saw them streaming down an open glen, the stag with its great antlers laid back and flying like the wind. So he shouted the Fian hunting-cry and rode furiously on their track. All day long they chased the stag through the echoing forest, and the fairy steed bore him unfaltering over rough ground and smooth, till at last as darkness began to fall the quarry was pulled down, and Oisín cut its throat with his hunting-knife. Long it seemed to him since he had felt glad and weary as he felt now, and since the woodland air with its odours of pine and mint and wild garlic had tasted so sweet in his mouth; and truly it was longer than he knew. But when he bade make ready the wood-oven for their meal, and build a bothy of boughs for their repose, Niam led him seven steps apart and seven to the left hand, and yet seven back to the place where they had killed the deer, and lo, there rose before him a stately Dún with litten windows and smoke drifting above its roof. When they entered, there was a table spread for a great company, and cooks and serving-men busy about a wide hearth where roast and boiled meats of every sort were being prepared. Casks of Greek wine stood open around the walls, and cups of gold were on the board. So they all ate and drank their sufficiency, and all night Oisín and Niam slept on a bed softer than swans-down in a chamber no less fair than that which they had in the City of the Land of Youth.

Next day, at the first light of dawn, they were on foot; and soon again the forest rang to the baying of hounds and the music of the hunting-horn. Oisín's steed bore him all day, tireless and swift as before, and again the quarry fell at night's approach, and again a palace rose in the wilderness for their night's entertainment, and all things in it even more abundant and more sumptuous than before. And so for seven days they fared in that forest, and seven stags were slain. Then Oisín grew wearied of hunting, and as he plunged his sharp black hunting-knife into the throat of the last stag, he thought of the sword of magic temper that hung idle by his side in the City of Youth, or rested from its golden nail in his bed-chamber, and he said to Niam, "Has thy father never a foe to tame, never a wrong to avenge? Surely the peasant is no man whose hand forgets the plough, nor the warrior whose hand forgets the sword hilt." Niam looked on him strangely for a while and as if she did not understand his words, or sought some meaning in them which yet she feared to find. But at last she said, "If deeds of arms be thy desire, Oisín, thou shalt have thy sufficiency ere long." And so they rode home, and slept that night in the palace of the City of Youth.

At daybreak on the following morn Niam roused Oisín, and she buckled on him his golden-hilted sword and his corselet of blue steel inlaid with gold. Then he put on his head a steel and gold helmet with dragon crest, and slung on his back a shield of bronze wrought all over with cunning hammer-work of serpentine lines that swelled and sank upon the surface, and coiled in mazy knots, or flowed in long sweeping curves like waves of the sea when they gather might and volume for their leap upon the sounding shore. In the glimmering dawn, through the empty streets of the fair city, they rode forth alone and took their way through fields of corn and by apple orchards where red fruit hung down to their hands. But by noontide their way began to mount upwards among blue hills that they had marked from the city walls toward the west, and of man's husbandry they saw no more, but tall red-stemmed pine trees bordered the way on either side, and silence and loneliness increased. At length they reached a broad table-land deep in the heart of the mountains, where nothing grew but long coarse grass, drooping by pools of black and motionless water, and where great boulders, bleached white or stained with slimy lichens of livid red, lay scattered far and wide about the plain. Against the sky the mountain line now showed like a threat of bared and angry teeth, and as they rode towards it Oisín perceived a huge fortress lying in the throat of a wide glen or mountain pass. White as death was the stone of which it was built, save where it was streaked with black or green from the foulness of wet mosses that clung to its cornices and battlements, and none seemed stirring about the place nor did any banner blow from its towers.

Then said Niam, "This, O Oisín, is the Dún of the giant Fovor of the Mighty Blows. In it he keeps prisoner a princess of the Fairy Folk whom he would fain make his bride, but he may not do so, nor may she escape, until Fovor has met in battle a champion who will undertake her cause. Approach, then, to the gate, if thou art fain to undertake this adventure, and blow the horn which hangs thereby, and then look to thy weapons, for soon indeed will the battle be broken upon thee."

Then Oisín rode to the gate and thrice he blew on the great horn which hung by it, and the clangour of it groaned drearily back from the cliffs that overhung the glen. Not thus indeed sounded the *Dord* of Finn as its call blew lust of fighting and scorn of death into the hearts of the Fianna amid the stress of battle. At the third blast the rusty gates opened, grinding on their hinges, and Oisín rode into a wide courtyard where servitors of evil aspect took his horse and Niam's, and led them into the hall of Fovor. Dark it was and low, with mouldering arras on its walls, and foul and withered rushes on the floor, where dogs gnawed the bones thrown to them at the last meal, and spilt ale and hacked fragments of flesh littered the bare oaken table. And here rose languidly to greet them a maiden bound with seven chains, to whom Niam spoke lovingly, saying that her champion was come and that her long captivity should end. And the maiden looked upon Oisín, whose proud bearing and jewelled armour made the mean place seem meaner still, and a light of hope and of joy seemed to glimmer upon her brow. So she gave them refreshment as she could, and afterwards they betook them once more to the courtyard, where the place of battle was set.

Here, at the further side, stood a huge man clad in rusty armour, who when he saw Oisín rushed upon him, silent and furious, and swinging a great battleaxe in his hand. But doubt and langour weighed upon Oisín's heart, and it seemed to him as if he were in an evil dream, which he knew was but a dream, and would be less than nothing when the hour of awakening should come. Yet he raised his shield and gripped the fairy sword, striving to shout the Fian battle-cry as he closed with Fovor. But soon a heavy blow smote him to the ground, and his armour clanged harshly on the stones. Then a cloud seemed to pass from his spirit, and he leaped to his feet quicker than an arrow flies from the string, and thrusting fiercely at the giant his sword-point gashed the under side of Fovor's arm when it was raised to strike, and Oisín saw his enemy's blood. Then the fight raged hither and thither about the wide courtyard, with trampling of feet and clash of steel and ringing of armour and shouts of onset as the heroes closed; Oisín, agile as a wild stag, evading the sweep of the mighty axe and rushing in with flickering blade at every unguarded moment, his whole soul bent on one fierce thought, to drive his point into some gap at shoulder or neck in Fovor's coat of mail. At length, when both were weary and wounded men, with hacked and battered armour, Oisín's blade cut the thong of Fovor's headpiece and it fell clattering to the ground. Another blow laid the giant prostrate, and Oisín leaned, dizzy and panting, upon his sword, while Fovor's serving-men took off their master in a litter, and Niam came to aid her lord. Then Oisín stripped off his armour in the great hall, and Niam tended to his wounds, healing them with magic herbs and murmured incantations, and they saw that one of the seven rusty chains that had bound the princess hung loose from its iron staple in the wall.

All night long Oisín lay in deep and healing slumber, and next day he arose, whole and strong, and hot to renew the fray. And the giant was likewise healed and his might and fierceness returned to him. So they fought till they were breathless and weary, and then to it again, and again, till in the end Oisín drove his sword to the hilt in the giant's shoulder where it joins the collar bone, and he fell aswoon, and was borne away as before. And another chain of the seven fell from the girdle of the captive maiden.

Thus for seven days went on the combat, and Oisín had seven nights of healing and rest, with the tenderness and beauty of Niam about his couch; and on the seventh day the maiden was free, and her folk brought her away, rejoicing, with banners and with music that made a brightness for a while in that forlorn and evil place.

But Oisín's heart was high with pride and victory, and a longing uprose in his heart with a rush like a springtide for the days when some great deed had been done among the Fianna, and the victors were hailed and lauded by the home-folk in the Dún of Allen, men and women leaving their toil or their pleasure to crowd round the heroes, and to question again and again, and to learn each thing that had passed; and the bards noting all to weave it into a glorious tale for after days; and more than all the smile and the look of Finn as he learned how his children had borne themselves in the face of death. And so Oisín said to Niam, "Let me, for a short while, return to the land of Erinn, that I may see there my friends and kin and tell them of the glory and joy that are mine in the Land of Youth." But Niam wept and laid her white arms about his neck, entreating him to think no more of the sad world where all men live and move under a canopy of death, and where summer is slain by winter, and youth by old age, and where love itself, if it die not by falsehood and wrong, perishes many a time of too complete a joy. But Oisín said, "The world of men compared with thy world is like this dreary waste compared with the city of thy father; yet in that city, Niam, none is better or worse than another, and I hunger to tell my tale to ignorant and feeble folk that my words can move, as words of mine have done of old, to wonder and delight. Then I shall return to thee, Niam, and to thy fair and blissful land; and having brought over to mortal men a tale that never man has told before, I shall be happy and at peace for ever in the Land of Youth."

So they fared back to the golden city, and next day Niam brought to Oisín the white steed that had borne them from Erinn, and bade him farewell. "This our steed," she said, "will carry thee across the sea to the land where I found thee, and whithersoever thou wilt, and what folk are there thou shalt see, and what tale thou hast to tell can be told. But never for even a moment must thou alight from his back, for if thy foot once touch again the soil of earth, thou shalt never win to me and to the Land of Youth again. And sorely do I fear some evil chance. Was not the love of Niam of the Head of Gold enough to fill a mortal's heart? But if thou must go, then go, and blessing and victory be thine."

Then Oisín held her long in his arms and kissed her, and vowed to make no long stay and never to alight from the fairy steed. And then he shook the golden reins and the horse threw its head aloft and snorted and bore him away in a pace like that of flowing water for speed and smoothness. Anon they came to the margin of the blue sea, and still the white steed galloped on, brushing the crests of the waves into glittering spray. The sun glared upon the sea and Oisín's head swam with the heat and motion, and in mist and dreams he rode where no day was, nor night, nor any thought of time, till at last his horse's hoofs ploughed through wet, yellow sands, and he saw black rocks rising up at each side of a little bay, and inland were fields green or brown, and white cottages thatched with reeds, and men and women, toil-worn and clad in earth-coloured garments, went to and fro about their tasks or stopped gazing at the rider in his crimson cloak and at the golden trappings of his horse. But among the cottages was a small house of stone such as Oisín had never seen in the land of Erinn; stone was its roof as well as the walls, very steep and high, and near-by from a rude frame of timber there hung a bell of bronze. Into this house there passed one whom from his shaven crown Oisín guessed to be a druid, and behind him two lads in white apparel. The druid having seen the horseman turned his eyes again to the ground and passed on, regarding him not, and the lads did likewise. And Oisín rode on, eager to reach the Dún upon the Hill of Allen and to see the faces of his kin and his friends.

At length, coming from the forest path into the great clearing where the Hill of Allen was wont to rise broad and green, with its rampart enclosing many white-walled dwellings, and the great hall towering high in the midst, he saw but grassy mounds overgrown with rank weeds and whin bushes, and among them pastured a peasant's kine.

Then a strange horror fell upon him, and he thought some enchantment from the land of Faery held his eyes and mocked him with false visions. He threw his arms abroad and shouted the names of Finn and Oscar, but none replied, and he thought that perchance the hounds might hear him, and he cried upon Bran and Sceolaun, and strained his ears if they might catch the faintest rustle or whisper of the world from the sight of which his eyes were holden, but he heard only the sigh of the wind in the whins. Then he rode in terror from that place, setting his face towards the eastern sea, for he meant to traverse Ireland from side to side and end to end in the search of some escape from his enchantment. But when he came near to the eastern sea and was now in the place which is called the Valley of the Thrushes,[24] he saw in a field upon the hillside a crowd of men striving to roll aside a great boulder from their tilled land, and an overseer directing them. Towards them he rode, meaning to ask them concerning Finn and the Fianna. As he came near, they all stopped their work to gaze upon him, for to them he appeared like a messenger of the Fairy Folk or an angel from heaven. Taller and mightier he was than the men-folk they knew, with sword-blue eyes and brown ruddy cheeks; in his mouth, as it were, a shower of pearls, and bright hair clustered beneath the rim of his helmet. And as Oisín looked upon their puny forms, marred by toil and care, and at the stone which they feebly strove to heave from its bed, he was filled with pity, and thought to himself, "not such were even the churls of Erinn when I left them for the Land of Youth," and he stooped from his saddle to help them. His hand he set to the boulder, and with a mighty heave he lifted it from where it lay and set it rolling down the hill. And the men raised a shout of wonder and applause, but their shouting changed in a moment into cries of terror and dismay, and they fled, jostling and overthrowing each other to escape from the place of fear; for a marvel horrible to see had taken place. For Oisín's saddle-girth had burst as he heaved the stone, and he fell headlong to the ground. In an instant the white steed had vanished from their eyes like a wreath of mist, and that which rose, feeble and staggering, from the ground was no youthful warrior but a man stricken with extreme old age, white-bearded and withered, who stretched out groping hands and moaned with feeble and bitter cries. And his crimson cloak and yellow silken tunic were now but coarse homespun stuff tied with a hempen girdle, and the gold-hilted sword was a rough oaken staff such as a beggar carries who wanders the roads from farmer's house to house.

When the people saw that the doom that had been wrought was not for them they returned, and found the old man prone on the ground with his face hidden in his arms. So they lifted him up and asked who he was and what had befallen him. Oisín gazed round on them with dim eyes, and at last he said, "I was Oisín the son of Finn, and I pray ye tell me where he now dwells, for his Dún on the Hill of Allen is now a desolation, and I have neither seen him nor heard his hunting horn from the Western to the Eastern Sea." Then the men gazed strangely on each other and on Oisín, and the overseer asked, "Of what Finn dost thou speak, for there be many of that name in Erinn?" Oisín said, "Surely of Finn mac Cumhal mac Trenmor, captain of the Fianna of Erinn." Then the overseer said, "Thou art daft, old man, and thou hast made us daft to take thee for a youth as we did a while agone. But we at least have now our wits again, and we know that Finn son of Cumhal and all his generation have been dead these three hundred years. At the battle of Gowra fell Oscar, son of Oisín, and Finn at the battle of Brea, as the historians tell us; and the lays of Oisín, whose death no man knows the manner of, are sung by our harpers at great men's feasts. But now the Talkenn,[25] Patrick, has come into Ireland and has preached to us the One God and Christ His Son, by whose might these old days and ways are done away with, and Finn and his Fianna, with their feasting and hunting and songs of war and of love, have no such reverence among us as the monks and virgins of holy Patrick, and the psalms and prayers that go up daily to cleanse us from sin and to save us from the fire of judgment." But Oisín replied, half hearing and still less comprehending what was said to him, "If thy God have slain Finn and Oscar, I would say that God is a strong man." Then they all cried out upon him, and some picked up stones, but the overseer bade them let him be until the Talkenn had spoken with him, and till he should order what was to be done.

So they brought him to Patrick, who entreated him gently and hospitably, and to Patrick he told the story of all that had befallen him. But Patrick bade his scribes write all carefully down, that the memory of the heroes whom Oisín had known, and of the joyous and free life they had led in the woods and glens and wild places of Erinn, should never be forgotten among men. And Oisín, during the short span of life that yet remained to him, told to Patrick many tales of the Fianna and their deeds, but of the three hundred years that he had spent with Niam in the Land of Youth he rarely spoke, for they seemed to him but as a vision or a dream of the night, set between a sunny and a rainy day.

CHAPTER XVI

THE HISTORY OF KING CORMAC

I

THE BIRTH OF CORMAC

Of all the kings that ruled over Ireland, none had a better and more loyal servant than was Finn mac Cumhal, and of all the captains and counsellors of kings none ever served a more glorious and a nobler monarch than did Finn, for the time that he served Cormac, son of Art, son of Conn of the Hundred Battles. At the time at which this monarch lived and reigned, the mist of sixteen centuries hangs between us and the history of Ireland, but through this mist there shine a few great and sunlike figures whose glory cannot be altogether hidden, and of these figures Cormac is the greatest and the brightest. Much that is told about him may be true, and much is certainly fable, but the fables themselves are a witness to his greatness; they are like forms seen in the mist when a great light is shining behind it, and we cannot always say when we are looking at the true light and when at the reflected glory.

The birth of Cormac was on this wise. His father, as we have said, was Art, son of Conn, and his mother was named Achta, being the daughter of a famous smith or ironworker of Connacht. Now before the birth of Cormac, Achta had a strange dream, namely, that her head was struck off from her body and that out of her neck there grew a great tree which extended its branches over all Ireland and flourished exceedingly, but a huge wave of the sea burst upon it and laid it low. Then from the roots of this tree there grew up another, but it did not attain the splendour of the first, and a blast of wind came from the West and overthrew it. On this the woman started from her sleep, and she woke her husband, Art, and told him her vision. "It is a true dream," said Art. "I am thy head, and this portends that I shall be violently taken from thee. But thou shalt bear me a son who shall be King of all Ireland, and shall rule with great power and glory until some disaster from the sea overtake him. But from him shall come yet another king, my grandson and thine, who shall also be cut down, and I think that the cause of his fall shall be the armies of the Fian host, who are swift and keen as the wind."

Not long thereafter Art, son of Conn, fell in battle with the Picts and Britons at the Plain of the Swine, which is between Athenry and Galway in Connacht. Now the leader of the invaders then was mac Con, a nephew to Art, who had been banished out of Ireland for rising against the High King; and when he had slain Art he seized the sovranty of Ireland and reigned there unlawfully for many years.

But before the battle, Art had counselled his wife:

"If things go ill with us in the fight, and I am slain, seek out my faithful friend Luna who dwells in Corann in Connacht, and he will protect thee till thy son be born." So Achta, with one maid, fled in her chariot before the host of mac Con and sought to go to the Dún of Luna. On her way thither, however, the hour came when her child should be born, and the maid turned the chariot aside into the wild wood at the place called Creevagh (the Place of the Twigs), and there, on a couch of twigs and leaves, she gave birth to a noble son.

Then Achta, when she had cherished her boy and rejoiced over him, bade her handmaid keep watch over both of them, and they fell asleep. But the maid's eyes were heavy with weariness and long travelling, and ere long she, too, was overpowered by slumber, and all three slept a deep sleep while the horses wandered away grazing through the wood.

By and by there came a she-wolf roaming through the wood in search of prey for her whelps, and it came upon the sleeping woman and the little child. It did not wake the woman, but very softly it picked up the infant and bore it off to the stony cave that is hard by to Creevagh in the hill that was afterwards called Mount Cormac.

After a while the mother waked up and found her child gone. Then she uttered a lamentable cry, and woke her handmaid, and both the women searched hither and thither, but no trace of the child could they find; and thus Luna found them; for he had heard news of the battle and the death of his King, and he had come to succour Achta as he had pledged his word to do. Luna and his men also made search for the infant, but in vain; and at last he conveyed the two sorrowing women to his palace; but Achta was somewhat comforted by her prophetic dream. Luna then proclaimed that whoever should discover the King's son, if he were yet alive, might claim of him what reward he would.

And so the time passed, till one day a man named Grec, a clansman of Luna the lord of Corann, as he ranged the woods hunting, came on a stony cavern in the side of a hill, and before it he saw wolf-cubs at play, and among them a naked child on all fours gambolling with them, and a great she-wolf that mothered them all. "Right," cried Grec, and off he goes to Luna his lord. "What wilt thou give me for the King's son?" said he. "What wilt thou have?" said Luna. So Grec asked for certain lands, and Luna bound himself to give them to him and to his posterity, and there lived and flourished the Clan Gregor for many a generation to come. So Luna, guided by Grec, went to the cave on Mount Cormac, and took the child and the wolf-cubs all together and brought them home. And the child they called Cormac, or the Chariot-Child. Now the lad grew up very comely and strong, and he abode with Luna in Connacht, and no one told him of his descent.

II

THE JUDGEMENT OF CORMAC

Once upon a time it happened that Cormac was at play with the two sons of Luna, and the lads grew angry in their play and came to blows, and Cormac struck one of them to the ground. "Sorrow on it," cried the lad, "here I have been beaten by one that knows not his clan or kindred, save that he is a fellow without a father." When Cormac heard that he was troubled and ashamed, and he went to Luna and told him what had been said.

And Luna seeing the trouble of the youth, and also that he was strong and noble to look on, and wise and eloquent in speech, held that the time was now come to reveal to him his descent. "Thou hadst indeed a clan and kindred," he said, "and a father of the noblest, for thou art the son of Art, the High King of Ireland, who was slain and dispossessed by mac Con. But it is foretold that thou shalt yet come to thy father's place, and the land pines for thee even now, for there is no good yield from earth or sea under the unlawful rule of him who now sits on the throne of Art."

"If that be so," said Cormac, "let us go to Tara, and bide our time there in my father's house."

So the two of them set out for Tara on the morrow morn. And this was the retinue they had with them: a body-guard of outlawed men that had revolted against mac Con and other lords and had gathered themselves together at Corann under Luna, and four wolves that had been cubs with Cormac when the she-wolf suckled him.

When they came to Tara, the folk there wondered at the fierce-eyed warriors and the grey beasts that played like dogs around Cormac, and the lad was adopted as a pupil by the King, to be taught arms and poetry and law. Much talk there was of his coming, and of his strange companions that are not wont to be the friends of man, and as the lad grew in comeliness and in knowledge the eyes of all were turned to him more and more, because the rule of mac Con was not good.

So the time wore on, till one day a case came for judgment before the King, in which the Queen sued a certain wealthy woman and an owner of herds named Benna, for that the sheep of Benna had strayed into the Queen's fields and had eaten to the ground a crop of woad[26] that was growing there. The King gave judgment, that the sheep which had eaten the woad were to be given to the Queen in compensation for what they had destroyed. Then Cormac rose up before the people and said, "Nay, but let the wool of the sheep, when they are next shorn, be given to the Queen, for the woad will grow again and so shall the wool." "A true judgment, a true judgment," cried all the folk that were present in the place; "a very king's son is he that hath pronounced it." And they murmured so loudly against mac Con that his druids counselled him to quit Tara lest a worse thing befall him. So he gave up the sovranty to Cormac and went southward into Munster to rally his friends there and recover the kingdom, and there he was slain by Cormac's men as he was distributing great largesse of gold and silver to his followers, in the place called The Field of the Gold.

So Cormac, son of Art, ruled in Tara and was High King of all Ireland. And the land, it is said, knew its rightful lord, and yielded harvests such as never were known, while the forest trees dripped with the abundance of honey and the lakes and rivers were alive with fish. So much game was there, too, that the folk could have lived on that alone and never put a ploughshare in the soil. In Cormac's time the autumn was not vexed with rain, nor the spring with icy winds, nor the summer with parching heat, nor the winter with whelming snows. His rule in Erinn, it is said, was like a wand of gold laid on a dish of silver.

Also he rebuilt the ramparts of Tara and made it strong, and he enlarged the great banqueting hall and made pillars of cedar in it ornamented with plates of bronze, and painted its lime-white walls in patterns of red and blue. Palaces for the women he also made there, and store-houses, and halls for the fighting men—never was Tara so populous or so glorious before or since. And for his wisdom and righteousness knowledge was given to him that none other in Ireland had as yet, for it was revealed to him that the Immortal Ones whom the Gael worshipped were but the names of One whom none can name, and that his message should ere long come to Ireland from over the eastern sea, calling the people to a sweeter and diviner faith.

And to the end of his life it was his way to have wolves about him, for he knew their speech and they his, and they were friendly and tame with him and his folk, since they were foster-brothers together in the wild wood.

III

THE MARRIAGE OF KING CORMAC

It happened that in Cormac's time there was a very wealthy farmer named Buicad[27] who dwelt in Leinster, and had vast herds of cattle and sheep and horses. This Buicad and his wife had no children, but they adopted a foster-child named Ethne, daughter of one Dunlang. Now Buicad was the most hospitable of men, and never refused aught to anyone, but he kept open house for all the nobles of Leinster who came with their following and feasted there as they would, day after day; and if any man fancied any of the cattle or other goods of Buicad, he might take them home with him, and none said him nay. Thus Buicad lived in great splendour, and his Dún was ever full to profusion with store of food and clothing and rich weapons, until in time it was all wasted away in boundless hospitality and generosity, and so many had had a share in his goods that they could never be recovered nor could it be said of any man that he was the cause of Buicad's undoing. But undone he was at last, and when there remained to him but one bull and seven cows he departed by night with his wife and Ethne from Dún Buicad, leaving his mansion desolate. And he travelled till he came to a place where there was a grove of oak trees by a little stream in the county of Meath, near where Cormac had a summer palace, and there he built himself a little hut and tended his few cattle, and Ethne waited as a maid-servant upon him and his wife.

Now on a certain day it happened that King Cormac rode out on horseback from his Dún in Meath, and in the course of his ride he came upon the little herd of Buicad towards evening, and he saw Ethne milking the cows. And this was the way she milked them: first she milked a portion of each cow's milk into a certain vessel, then she took a second vessel and milked into it the remaining portion, in which was the richest cream, and these two vessels she kept apart. Cormac watched all this. She then bore the vessels of milk into the hut, and came out again with two other vessels and a small cup. These she bore down to the river-side; and one of the vessels she filled by means of the cup from the water at the brink of the stream,

93

but the other vessel she bore out into the middle of the stream and there filled it from the deepest of the running water. After this she took a sickle and began cutting rushes by the river-side, and Cormac saw that when she cut a wisp of long rushes she would put it on one side, and the short rushes on the other, and she bore them separately into the house. But Cormac stopped her and saluted her, and said:

"For whom, maiden, art thou making this careful choice of the milk and the rushes and the water?"

"I am making it," said she, "for one who is worthy that I should do far more than that for him, if I could."

"What is his name?"

"Buicad, the farmer," said Ethne.

"Is it that Buicad, who was the rich farmer in Leinster that all Ireland has heard of?" asked the King.

"It is even so."

"Then thou art his foster-child, Ethne the daughter of Dunlang?" said Cormac.

"I am," said Ethne.

"Wilt thou be my wife and Queen of Erinn?" then said Cormac.

"If it please my foster-father to give me to thee, O King, I am willing," replied Ethne. Then Cormac took Ethne by the hand and they went before Buicad, and he consented to give her to Cormac to wife. And Buicad was given rich lands and great store of cattle in the district of Odran close by Tara, and Ethne the Queen loved him and visited him so long as his life endured.

IV

THE INSTRUCTIONS OF THE KING

Ethne bore to Cormac a son, her firstborn, named Cairbry, who was King of Ireland after Cormac. It was during the lifetime of Cormac that Cairbry came to the throne, for it happened that ere he died Cormac was wounded by a chance cast of a spear and lost one of his eyes, and it was forbidden that any man having a blemish should be a king in Ireland. Cormac therefore gave up the kingdom into the hands of Cairbry, but before he did so he told his son all the wisdom that he had in the governing of men, and this was written down in a book which is called *The Instructions of Cormac*.[28] These are among the things which are found in it, of the wisdom of Cormac:—

Let him (the king) restrain the great,
Let him exalt the good,
Let him establish peace,
Let him plant law,
Let him protect the just,
Let him bind the unjust,
Let his warriors be many and his counsellors few,
Let him shine in company and be the sun of the mead-hall,

94

Let him punish with a full fine wrong done knowingly,
and with a half-fine wrong done in ignorance.

Cairbry said, "What are good customs for a tribe to pursue?" "They are as follows," replied Cormac:—

"To have frequent assemblies,
To be ever enquiring, to question the wise men,
To keep order in assemblies,
To follow ancient lore,
Not to crush the miserable,
To keep faith in treaties,
To consolidate kinship,
Fighting-men not to be arrogant,
To keep contracts faithfully,
To guard the frontiers against every ill."

"Tell me, O Cormac," said Cairbry, "what are good customs for the giver of a feast?" and Cormac said:—

"To have lighted lamps,
To be active in entertaining the company,
To be liberal in dispensing ale,
To tell stories briefly,
To be of joyous countenance,
To keep silence during recitals."

"Tell me, O Cormac," said his son once, "what were thy habits when thou wert a lad?" And Cormac said:—

"I was a listener in woods,
I was a gazer at stars,
I pried into no man's secrets,
I was mild in the hall,
I was fierce in the fray,
I was not given to making promises,
I reverenced the aged,
I spoke ill of no man in his absence,
I was fonder of giving than of asking."

"If you listen to my teaching," said Cormac:—

"Do not deride any old person though you be young
Nor any poor man though you be rich,
Nor any naked though you be well-clad,
Nor any lame though you be swift,
Nor any blind though you be keen-sighted,
Nor any invalid though you be robust,
Nor any dull though you be clever,
Nor any fool though you be wise.

"Yet be not slothful, nor fierce, nor sleepy, nor niggardly, nor feckless nor envious, for all these are hateful before God and men.

"Do not join in blasphemy, nor be the butt of an assembly; be not moody in an alehouse, and never forget a tryst."

"What are the most lasting things on earth?" asked Cairbry.

"Not hard to tell," said Cormac; "they are grass, copper, and a yew-tree."

"If you will listen to me," said Cormac, "this is my instruction for the management of your household and your realm:—

"Let not a man with many friends be your steward,
Nor a woman with sons and foster-sons your housekeeper,
Nor a greedy man your butler,
Nor a man of much delay your miller,
Nor a violent, foul-mouthed man your messenger,
Nor a grumbling sluggard your servant,
Nor a talkative man your counsellor,
Nor a tippler your cup-bearer,
Nor a short-sighted man your watchman,
Nor a bitter, haughty man your doorkeeper,
Nor a tender-hearted man your judge,
Nor an ignorant man your leader,
Nor an unlucky man your counsellor."

Such were the counsels that Cormac mac Art gave to his son Cairbry. And Cairbry became King after his father's abdication, and reigned seven and twenty years, till he and Oscar, son of Oisín, slew one another at the battle of Gowra.

V

CORMAC SETS UP THE FIRST MILL IN ERINN

During the reign of Cormac it happened that some of the lords of Ulster made a raid upon the Picts in Alba[29] and brought home many captives. Among them was a Pictish maiden named Kiernit, daughter of a king of that nation, who was strangely beautiful, and for that the Ulstermen sent her as a gift to King Cormac. And Cormac gave her as a household slave to his wife Ethne, who set her to grinding corn with a hand-quern, as women in Erinn were used to do. One day as Cormac was in the palace of the Queen he saw Kiernit labouring at her task and weeping as she wrought, for the toil was heavy and she was unused to it. Then Cormac was moved with compassion for the women that ground corn throughout Ireland, and he sent to Alba for artificers to come over and set up a mill, for up to then there were no mills in Ireland. Now there was in Tara, as there is to this day, a well of water called *The Pearly*, for the purity and brightness of the water that sprang from it, and it ran in a stream down the hillside, as it still runs, but now only in a slender trickle. Over this stream Cormac bade them build the first mill that was in Ireland, and the bright water turned the wheel merrily round, and the women in Tara toiled at the quern no more.

VI

A PLEASANT STORY OF CORMAC'S BREHON

Among other affairs which Cormac regulated for himself and all kings who should come after him was the number and quality of the officers who should be in constant attendance on the King. Of these he ordained that there should be ten, to wit one lord, one brehon, one druid, one physician, one bard, one historian, one musician and three stewards. The function of the brehon, or judge, was to know the ancient customs and the laws of Ireland, and to declare them to the King whenever any matter relating to them came before him. Now Cormac's chief brehon was at first one Fithel. But Fithel's time came to die, and his son Flahari,[30] a wise and learned man, trained by his father in all the laws of the Gael, was to be brehon to the High King in his father's stead. Fithel then called his son to his bedside and said:—

"Thou art well acquainted, my son, with all the laws and customs of the Gael, and worthy to be the chief brehon of King Cormac. But wisdom of life thou hast not yet obtained, for it is written in no law-book. This thou must learn for thyself, from life itself; yet somewhat of it I can impart unto thee, and it will keep thee in the path of safety, which is not easily trodden by those who are in the counsels of great kings. Mark now these four precepts, and obey them, and thou wilt avoid many of the pit-falls in thy way:—

"Take not a king's son in fosterage,[31]
Impart no dangerous secret to thy wife,
Raise not the son of a serf to a high position,
Commit not thy purse or treasure to a sister's keeping."

Having said this Fithel died, and Flahari became chief brehon in his stead.

After a time Flahari thought to himself, "I am minded to test my father's wisdom of life and to see if it be true wisdom or but wise-seeming babble. For knowledge is no knowledge until it be tried by life."

So he went before the King and said, "If thou art willing, Cormac, I would gladly have one of thy sons in fosterage." At this Cormac was well pleased, and a young child of the sons of Cormac was given to Flahari to bring up, and Flahari took the child to his own Dún, and there began to nurture and to train him as it was fitting.

After a time, however, Flahari one day took the child by the hand and went with him into the deep recesses of the forest where dwelt one of the swine-herds who minded the swine of Flahari. To him Flahari handed over the child and bade him guard him as the apple of his eye, and to be ready deliver him up again when he was required. The Flahari went home, and for some days went about like a man weighed down by gloomy and bitter thoughts. His wife marked that, and sought to know the reason, but Flahari put her off. At last when she continually pressed him to reveal the cause of his trouble, he said "If them must needs learn what ails me, and if thou canst keep a secret full of danger to me and thee, know that I am gloomy and distraught because I have killed the son of Cormac." At this the woman cried out, "Murderer parricide, hast thou spilled the King's blood, and shall Cormac not know it, and do justice on thee?" And she sent word to Cormac that he should come and seize her husband for that crime.

But before the officers came, Flahari took a young man, the son of his butler, and placed him in charge of his lands to manage them, while Flahari was away for his trial at Tara. And he also gave to his sister a treasure of gold and silver to keep for him, lest it should be made a spoil of while he was absent. Then he went with the officers to Tara, denying his offence and his confession, but when Cormac had heard all, and the child could not be found, he sentenced him to be put to death.

Flahari then sent a messenger to his sister, begging her to send him at once a portion of the treasure he had left with her, that he might use it to make himself friends among the folk at court, and perchance obtain a remission of his sentence; but she sent the messenger back again empty, saying she knew not of what he spoke.

On this Flahari deemed that the time was come to reveal the truth, so he obtained permission from the King to send a message to his swineherd before he died, and to hear the man's reply. And the message was this, that Murtach the herd should come without delay to Tara and bring with him the child that Flahari had committed to him. Howbeit this messenger also came back empty, and reported that on reaching Dún Flahari he had been met by the butler's son that was over the estate, who had questioned him of his errand, and had then said, "Murtach the serf has run away as soon as he heard of his lord's downfall, and if he had any child in his care he has taken it away with him, and he cannot be found." This he said because, on hearing of the child, he guessed what this might mean, and he had been the bitterest of all in urging Flahari's death, hoping to be rewarded with a share of his lands.

Then Flahari said to himself, "Truly the proving of my father's wisdom of life has brought me very near to death." So he sent for the King and entreated him that he might be suffered to go himself to the dwelling of Murtach the herd, promising that the King's son should be then restored to him, "or if not," said he, "let me then be slain there without more ado." With great difficulty Cormac was moved to consent to this, for he believed it was but a subterfuge of Flahari's to put off the evil day or perchance to find a way of escape. But next day Flahari was straitly bound and set in a chariot, and, with a guard of spearmen about him and Cormac himself riding behind, they set out for Dún Flahari. Then Flahari guided them through the wild wood till at last they came to the clearing where stood the dwelling of Murtach the swineherd, and lo! there was the son of Cormac playing merrily before the door. And the child ran to his foster-father to kiss him, but when he saw Flahari in bonds he burst out weeping and would not be at peace until he was set free.

Then Murtach slew one of the boars of his herd and made an oven in the earth after the manner of the Fianna, and made over it a fire of boughs that he had drying in a shed. And when the boar was baked he set it before the company with ale and mead in methers of beechwood, and they all feasted and were glad of heart.

Cormac then asked of Flahari why he had suffered himself to be brought into this trouble. "I did so," said Flahari, "to prove the four counsels which my father gave them ere he died, and I have proved them and found them to be wise. In the first place, it is not wise for any man that is not a king to take the fosterage of a king's son, for if aught shall happen to the lad, his own life is in the king's hands and with his life he shall answer for it. Secondly, the keeping of a secret, said my father, is not in the nature of women in general, therefore no dangerous secret should be entrusted to them. The third counsel my father gave me was not to raise up or enrich the son of a serf, for such persons are apt to forget benefits conferred on them, and moreover it irks them that he who raised them up should know the poor estate from which they sprang. And good, too, is the fourth counsel my father gave me, not to entrust my treasure to my sister, for it is the nature of most women to regard as spoil any valuables that are entrusted to them to keep for others."

VII

THE JUDGEMENT CONCERNING CORMAC'S SWORD

When Cormac, son of Art, son of Conn of the Hundred Battles, was High King in Erinn, great was the peace and splendour of his reign, and no provincial king or chief in any part of the country lifted up his head against Cormac. At his court in Tara were many noble youths, who were trained up there in all matters befitting their rank and station.

One of these youths was named Socht, son of Fithel. Socht had a wonderful sword, named "The Hard-headed Steeling," which was said to have been long ago the sword of Cuchulain. It had a hilt of gold and a belt of silver, and its point was double-edged. At night it shone like a candle. If its point were bent back to the hilt it would fly back again and be as straight as before. If it was held in running water and a hair were floated down against the edge, it would sever the hair. It was a saying that this sword would make two halves of a man, and for a while he would not perceive what had befallen him. This sword was held by Socht for a tribal possession from father and grandfather.

There was at this time a famous steward to the High King in Tara whose name was Dubdrenn. This man asked Socht to sell him the sword. He promised to Socht such a ration as he, Dubdrenn, had every night, and four men's food for the family of Socht, and, after that, Socht to have the full value of the sword at his own appraisement. "No," said Socht. "I may not sell my father's treasures while he is alive."

And thus they went on, Dubdrenn's mind ever running on the sword. At last he bade Socht to a drinking-bout, and plied him so with wine and mead that Socht became drunken, and knew not where he was, and finally fell asleep.

Then the steward takes the sword and goes to the King's brazier, by name Connu.

"Art thou able," says Dubdrenn, "to open the hilt of this sword?" "I am that," says the brazier.

Then the brazier took apart the hilt, and within, upon the tang of the blade, he wrote the steward's name, even Dubdrenn, and the steward laid the sword again by the side of Socht.

So it was for three months after that, and the steward continued to ask Socht to sell him the sword, but he could not get it from him.

Then the steward brought a suit for the sword before the High King, and he claimed that it was his own and that it had been taken from him. But Socht declared that the sword was his by long possession and by equity, and he would not give it up.

Then Socht went to his father, Fithel the brehon, and begged him to take part in the action and to defend his claim. But Fithel said, "Nay, thou art too apt to blame the pleadings of other men; plead for thyself."

So the court was set, and Socht was called upon to prove that the sword was his. He swore that it was a family treasure, and thus it had come down to him.

The steward said, "Well, O Cormac, the oath that Socht has uttered is a lie."

"What proof hast thou of that?" asked Cormac.

"Not hard to declare," replied the steward. "If the sword be mine, my name stands graved therein, concealed within the hilt of the sword."

"That will soon be known," says Cormac, and therewith he had the brazier summoned. The brazier comes and breaks open the hilt and the name of Dubdrenn stands written within it. Thus a dead thing testified in law against a living man.

Then Socht said, "Hear ye, O men of Erinn and Cormac the King! I acknowledge that this man is the owner of the sword." And to Dubdrenn he said, "The property therein and all the obligations of it pass from me to thee."

Dubdrenn said, "I acknowledge property in the sword and all its obligations."

Then said Socht, "This sword was found in the neck of my grandfather Angus, and till this day it never was known who had done that murder. Do justice, O King, for this crime."

Said the King to Dubdrenn, "Thou art liable for more than the sword is worth." So he awarded to Socht the price of seven bondwomen as blood-fine for the slaying of Angus, and restitution of the sword to Socht. Then the steward confessed the story of the sword, and Cormac levied seven other cumals from the brazier. But Cormac said, "This is in truth the sword of Cuchulain, and by it was slain my grandfather, even Conn of the Hundred Battles, at the hands of the King of Ulster, of whom it is written:—

"With a host, with a valiant band
Well did he go into Connacht.
Alas, that he saw the blood of Conn
On the side of Cuchulain's sword!"

Then Cormac and Fithel agreed that the sword be given to Cormac as blood-fine for the death of Conn, and his it was; and it was the third best of the royal treasures that were in Erin: namely, Cormac's Cup, that broke if a falsehood were spoken over it and became whole if a truth were spoken; and the Bell Branch that he got in Fairyland, whose music when it was shaken would put to sleep wounded men, and women in travail; and the Sword of Cuchulain, against which, and against the man that held it in his hand, no victory could ever be won.

VIII

THE DISAPPEARANCE OF CORMAC

In the chronicle of the Kings of Ireland that was written by Tierna the Historian in the eleventh century after Christ's coming, there is noted down in the annals of the year 248, "Disappearance of Cormac, grandson of Conn, for seven months." That which happened to Cormac during these seven months is told in one of the bardic stories of Ireland, being the Story of Cormac's Journey to Fairyland, and this was the manner of it.

One day Cormac, son of Art, was looking over the ramparts of his royal Dún of Tara, when he saw a young man, glorious to look on in his person and his apparel, coming towards him across the plain of Bregia. The young man bore in his hand, as it were, a branch, from which hung nine golden bells formed like apples. When he shook the branch the nine apples beat against each other and made music so sweet that there was no pain or sorrow in the world that a man would not forget while he hearkened to it.

"Does this branch belong to thee?" asked Cormac of the youth.

"Truly it does," replied the youth.

"Wilt thou sell it to me?" said Cormac.

"I never had aught that I would not sell for a price," said the young man.

"What is thy price?" asked Cormac.

"The price shall be what I will," said the young man.

"I will give thee whatever thou desirest of all that is mine," said Cormac, for he coveted the branch exceedingly, and the enchantment was heavy upon him.

So the youth gave him the bell-branch, and then said, "My price is thy wife and thy son and thy daughter."

Then they went together into the palace and found there Cormac's wife and his children. "That is a wonderful jewel thou hast in thy hand, Cormac," said Ethne.

"It is," said Cormac, "and great is the price I have paid for it."

"What is that price?" said Ethne.

"Even thou and thy children twain," said the King.

"Never hast thou done such a thing," cried Ethne, "as to prefer any treasure in the world before us three!" And they all three lamented and implored, but Cormac shook the branch and immediately their sorrow was forgotten, and they went away willingly with the young man across the plain of Bregia until a mist hid them from the eyes of Cormac. And when the people murmured and complained against Cormac, for Ethne and her children were much beloved of them, Cormac shook the bell-branch and their grief was turned into joy.

A year went by after this, and then Cormac longed for his wife and children again, nor could the bell-branch any longer bring him forgetfulness of them. So one morning he took the branch and went out alone from Tara over the plain, taking the direction in which they had passed away a year agone; and ere long little wreathes of mist began to curl about his feet, and then to flit by him like long trailing robes, and he knew no more where he was. After a time, however, he came out again into sunshine and clear sky, and found himself in a country of flowery meadows and of woods filled with singing-birds where he had never journeyed before. He walked on, till at last he came to a great and stately mansion with a crowd of builders at work upon it, and they were roofing it with a thatch made of the wings of strange birds. But when they had half covered the house, their supply of feathers ran short, and they rode off in haste to seek for more. While they were gone, however, a wind arose and whirled away the feathers already laid on, so that the rafters were left bare as before. And this happened again and again, as Cormac gazed on them for he knew not how long. At last his patience left him and he said, "I see with that ye have been doing this since the beginning of the world, and that ye will still be doing it in the end thereof," and with that he went on his way.

And many other strange things he saw, but of them we say nothing now, till he came to the gateway of a great and lofty Dún, where he entered in and asked hospitality. Then there came to him a tall man clad in a cloak of blue that changed into silver or to purple as its folds waved in the light, and with him was a woman more beautiful than the daughters of men, even she of whom it was said her beauty was as that of a tear when it drops from the eyelid, so crystal-pure it was and bright.[32] They greeted Cormac courteously and begged him to stay with them for the night.

Cormac then entered a great hall with pillars of cedar and many-coloured silken hangings on the walls. In the midst of it was a fire-place whereon the host threw a huge log, and shortly afterwards brought in a young pig which Cormac cut up to roast before the fire. He first put one quarter of the pig to roast, and then his host said to him,

"Tell us a tale, stranger, and if it be a true one the quarter will be done as soon as the tale is told."

"Do thou begin," said Cormac, "and then thy wife, and after that my turn will come."

"Good," said the host. "This is my tale. I have seven of these swine, and with their flesh the whole world could be fed. When one of them is killed and eaten, I need but put its bones into the pig-trough and on the morrow it is alive and well again." They looked at the fireplace, and behold, the first quarter of the pig was done and ready to be served.

Then Cormac put on the second quarter, and the woman took up her tale. "I have seven white cows," she said, "and seven pails are filled with the milk of them each day. Though all the folk in the world were gathered together to drink of this milk, there would be enough and to spare for all." As soon as she had said that, they saw that the second quarter of the pig was roasted.

Then Cormac said: "I know you now, who you are; for it is Mananan that owns the seven swine of Faery, and it is out of the Land of Promise that he fetched Fand his wife and her seven cows." Then immediately the third quarter of the pig was done.

"Tell us now," said Mananan, "who thou art and why thou art come hither."

Cormac then told his story, of the branch with its nine golden apples and how he had bartered for it his wife and his children, and he was now-seeking them through the world. And when he had made an end, the last quarter of the pig was done.

"Come, let us set to the feast," then said Mananan; but Cormac said, "Never have I sat down to meat in a company of two only." "Nay," said Mananan, "but there are more to come." With that he opened a door in the hall and in it appeared Queen Ethne and her two children. And when they had embraced and rejoiced in each other Mananan said, "It was I who took them from thee, Cormac, and who gave thee the bell-branch, for I wished to bring thee hither to be my guest for the sake of thy nobleness and thy wisdom."

Then they all sat down to table and feasted and made merry, and when they had satisfied themselves with meat and drink, Mananan showed the wonders of his household to King Cormac. And he took up a golden cup which stood on the table, and said: "This cup hath a magical property, for if a lie be spoken over it, it will immediately break in pieces, and if a truth be spoken it will be made whole again." "Prove this to me," said Cormac. "That is easily done," said Mananan. "Thy wife hath had a new husband since I carried her off from thee." Straightway the cup fell apart into four pieces. "My husband has lied to thee, Cormac," said Fand, and immediately the cup became whole again.

Cormac then began to question Mananan as to the things he had seen on his way thither, and he told him of the house that was being thatched with the wings of birds, and of the men that kept returning ever and again to their work as the wind destroyed it. And Mananan said, "These, O Cormac, are the men of art, who seek to gather together much money and gear of all kinds by the exercise of their craft, but as fast as they get it, so they spend it, or faster and the result is that they will never be rich." But when he had said this it is related that the golden cup broke into pieces where it stood. Then Cormac said, "The explanation thou hast given of this mystery is not true." Mananan smiled, and said, "Nevertheless it must suffice thee, O King, for the truth of this matter may not be known, lest the men of art give over the roofing of the house and it be covered with common thatch."

So when they had talked their fill, Cormac and his wife and children were brought to a chamber where they lay down to sleep. But when they woke up on the morrow morn, they found themselves in the Queen's chamber in the royal palace of Tara, and by Cormac's side were found the bell-branch and the magical cup and the cloth of gold that had covered the table where they sat in the palace of Mananan. Seven months it was since Cormac had gone out from Tara to search for his wife and children, but it seemed to him that he had been absent but for the space of a single day and night.

IX

DESCRIPTION OF CORMAC[33]

"A noble and illustrious king assumed the sovranty and rule of Erinn, namely Cormac, grandson of Conn of the Hundred Battles. The world was full of all goodness in his time; there were fruit and fatness of the land, and abundant produce of the sea, with peace and ease and happiness. There were no killings or plunderings in his time, but everyone occupied his land in happiness.

"The nobles of Ireland assembled to drink the Banquet of Tara with Cormac at a certain time.... Magnificently did Cormac come to this great Assembly; for no man, his equal in beauty, had preceded him, excepting Conary Mór or Conor son of Caffa, or Angus Óg son of the Dagda.[34] Splendid, indeed, was Cormac's appearance in that Assembly. His hair was slightly curled, and of golden colour; a scarlet shield he had, with engraved devices, and golden bosses and ridges of silver. A wide-folding purple cloak was on him with a gem-set gold brooch over his breast; a golden torque round his neck; a white-collared shirt embroidered with gold was on him; a girdle with golden buckles and studded with precious stones was around him; two golden net-work sandals with golden buckles upon his feet; two spears with golden sockets and many red bronze rivets in his hand; while he stood in the full glow of beauty, without defect or blemish. You would think it was a shower of pearls that was set in his mouth, his lips were rubies, his symmetrical body was as white as snow, his cheek was ruddy as the berry of the mountain-ash, his eyes were like the sloe, his brows and eye-lashes were like the sheen of a blue-black lance."

X

THE DEATH AND BURIAL OF CORMAC

Strange was the birth and childhood of Cormac strange his life and strange the manner of his death and burial, as we now have to narrate.

Cormac, it is said, was the third man in Ireland who heard of the Christian Faith before the coming of Patrick. One was Conor mac Nessa, King of Ulster, whose druid told him of the crucifixion of Christ and who died of that knowledge.[35] The second was the wise judge, Morann, and the third Cormac, son of Art. This knowledge was revealed to him by divine illumination, and thenceforth he refused to consult the druids or to worship the images which they made as emblems of the Immortal Ones.

One day it happened that Cormac after he had laid down the kingship of Ireland, was present when the druids and a concourse of people were worshipping the great golden image which was set up in the plain called Moy Slaught. When the ceremony was done, the chief druid, whose name was Moylann, spoke to Cormac and said: "Why, O Cormac, didst thou not bow down and adore the golden image of the god like the rest of the people?"

And Cormac said: "Never will I worship a stock[36] that my own carpenter has made. Rather would I worship the man that made it, for he is nobler than the work of his hands."

Then it is told that Moylann by magic art caused the image to move and leap before the eyes of Cormac. "Seest thou that?" said Moylann.

"Although I see," said Cormac, "I will do no worship save to the God of Heaven and Earth and Hell."

Then Cormac went to his own home at Sletty on the Boyne, for there he lived after he had given up the kingdom to his son Cairbry. But the druids of Erinn came together and consulted over this matter, and they determined solemnly to curse Cormac and invoke the vengeance of their gods upon him lest the people should think that any man could despise and reject their gods, and suffer no ill for it.

So they cursed Cormac in his flesh and bones, in his waking and sleeping, in his down sitting and his uprising, and each day they turned over the Wishing Stone upon the altar of their god,[37] and wove mighty spells against his life. And whether it was that these took effect, or that the druids prevailed upon some traitorous servant of Cormac's to work their will, so it was that he died not long thereafter; and some say that he was choked by a fish bone as he sat at meat in his house at Sletty on the Boyne.

But when he felt his end approaching, and had still the power to speak, he said to those that gathered round his bed:—

"When I am gone I charge you that ye bury me not at Brugh of the Boyne where is the royal cemetery of the Kings of Erinn.[38] For all these kings paid adoration to gods of wood or stone, or to the Sun and the Elements, whose signs are carved on the walls of their tombs, but I have learned to know the One God, immortal, invisible, by whom the earth and heavens were made. Soon there will come into Erinn one from the East who will declare Him unto us, and then wooden gods and cursing priests shall plague us no longer in this land. Bury me then not at Brugh-na-Boyna, but on the hither-side of Boyne, at Ross-na-ree, where there is a sunny, eastward-sloping hill, there would I await the coming of the sun of truth."

So spake Cormac, and he died, and there was a very great mourning for him in the land. But when the time came for his burial, the princes and lords of the Gael vowed that he should lie in Brugh with Art, his father, and Conn of the Hundred Battles, and many another king, in the great stone chambers of the royal dead. For Ross-na-ree, they said, is but a green hill of no note; and Cormac's expectation of the message of the new God they took to be but the wanderings of a dying man.

Now Brugh-na-Boyna lay at the farther side of the Boyne from Sletty, and near by was a shallow ford where the river could be crossed. But when the funeral train came down to the ford, bearing aloft the body of the King, lo! the river had risen as though a tempest had burst upon it at its far-off sources in the hills, and between them and the farther bank was now a broad and foaming flood, and the stakes that marked the ford were washed clean away. Even so they made trial of the ford, and thrice the bearers waded in and thrice they were forced to turn back lest the flood should sweep them down. At length six of the tallest and mightiest of the warriors of the High King took up the bier upon their shoulders, and strode in. And first the watchers on the bank saw the brown water swirl about their knees, and then they sank thigh-deep, and at last it foamed against their shoulders, yet still they braced themselves against the current, moving forward very slowly as they found foothold among the slippery rocks in the river-bed. But when they had almost reached the mid-stream it seemed as if a great surge overwhelmed them, and caught the bier from their shoulders as they plunged and clutched around it, and they must needs make back for the shore as best they could, while Boyne swept down the body of Cormac to the sea.

On the following morning, however, shepherds driving their flocks to pasture on the hillside of Ross-na-ree found cast upon the shore the body of an aged man of noble countenance, half wrapped in a silken pall; and knowing not who this might be they dug a grave in the grassy hill, and there laid the stranger, and laid the green sods over him again.

There still sleeps Cormac the King, and neither Ogham-lettered stone nor sculptured cross marks his solitary grave. But he lies in the place where he would be, of which a poet of the Gael in our day has written:—

"A tranquil spot: a hopeful sound
Comes from the ever-youthful stream, And still on daisied mead and mound
The dawn delays with tenderer beam.

"Round Cormac, spring renews her buds:
In march perpetual by his side Down come the earth-fresh April floods,
And up the sea-fresh salmon glide;

"And life and time rejoicing run
From age to age their wonted way; But still he waits the risen sun,
For still 'tis only dawning day."[39]

Notes on the Sources

The Story of the Children of Lir and *The Quest of the Sons of Turenn* are two of the three famous and popular tales entitled "The Three Sorrows of Storytelling." The third is the *Tragedy of the Sons of Usna*, rendered by Miss Eleanor Hull in her volume CUCHULAIN. I have taken the two stories which are given here from the versions in modern Irish published by the Society for the Preservation of the Irish Language, with notes and translation. Neither of them is found in any very early MS., but their subject-matter certainly goes back to very primitive times.

The Secret of Labra is taken from Keating's FORUS FEASA AR EIRINN, edited with translation by the Rev. P.S. Dineen for the Irish Texts Society, vol. i. p. 172.

The Carving of mac Datho's Boar. This is a clean, fierce, fighting story, notable both for its intensely dramatic *dénouement*, and for the complete absence from it of the magical or supernatural element which is so common a feature in Gaelic tales. It has been edited and translated from one MS. by Dr Kuno Meyer, in *Hibernica Minora* (ANECDOTA OXONIENSIA), 1894, and translated from THE BOOK OF LEINSTER (twelfth century) in Leahy's HEROIC ROMANCES.

The Vengeance of Mesgedra. This story, as I have given it, is a combination of two tales, *The Siege of Howth* and *The Death of King Conor*. The second really completes the first, though they are not found united in Irish literature. Both pieces are given in O'Curry's MS. MATERIALS OF IRISH HISTORY, and Miss Hull has printed translations of them in her CUCHULLIN SAGA, the translation of the *Siege* being by Dr Whitly Stokes and that of the *Death of Conor* by O'Curry. These are very ancient tales and contain a strong barbaric element. Versions of both of them are found in the great MS. collection known as the BOOK OF LEINSTER (twelfth century).

King Iubdan and King Fergus is a brilliant piece of fairy literature. The imaginative grace, the humour, and, at the close, the tragic dignity of this tale make it worthy of being much more widely known than it has yet become. The original, taken from one of the Egerton MSS. in the British Museum, will be found with a translation in O'Grady's SILVA GADELICA. For the conclusion, I have in the main followed another version (containing the death of Fergus only), given in the SEANCUS MOR and finely versified by Sir Samuel Ferguson in his POEMS, 1880.

The Story of Etain and Midir. This beautiful and very ancient romance is extant in two distinct versions, both of which are translated by Mr A.H. Leahy in his HEROIC ROMANCES. The tale is found in several MSS., among others, in the twelfth century BOOK OF THE DUN COW (LEABHAR NA H-UIDHRE). It has been recently made the subject of a dramatic poem by "Fiona Macleod."

How Ethne quitted Fairyland is taken from D'Arbois de Jubainville's CYCLE MYTHOLOGIQUE IRLANDAIS, ch. xii. 4. The original is to be found in the fifteenth century MS., entitled THE BOOK OF FERMOY.

The Boyhood of Finn is based chiefly on the MACGNIOMHARTHA FHINN, published in 1856, with a translation, in the *TRANSACTIONS OF THE OSSIANIC SOCIETY*, vol. iv. I am also indebted, particularly for the translation of the difficult *Song of Finn in Praise of May*, to Dr Kuno Meyer's translation published in *Ériu* (the Journal of the School of Irish Learning), vol. i. pt. 2.

The Coming of Finn, Finns Chief Men, the *Tale of Vivionn* and *The Chase of the Gilla Dacar*, are all handfuls from that rich mine of Gaelic literature, Mr Standish Hayes O'Grady's SILVA GADELICA. In the *Gilla Dacar* I have modified the second half of the story rather freely. It appears to have been originally an example of a well-known class of folk-tales dealing with the subject of the Rescue of Fairyland. The same motive occurs in the famous tale called *The Sickbed of Cuchulain*. The idea is that some fairy potentate, whose realm is invaded and oppressed, entices a mortal champion to come to his aid and rewards him with magical gifts. But the eighteenth century narrator whose MS. was edited by Mr S.H. O'Grady, apparently had not the clue to the real meaning of his material, and after going on brilliantly up to the point where Dermot plunges into the magic well, he becomes incoherent, and the rest of the tale is merely a string of episodes having no particular connexion with each other or with the central theme. The latter I have here endeavoured to restore to view. The *Gilla Dacar* is given from another Gaelic version by Dr P.W. Joyce in his invaluable book, OLD CELTIC ROMANCES.

The Birth of Oisín I have found in Patrick Kennedy's LEGENDARY FICTIONS OF THE IRISH CELTS. I do not know the Gaelic original.

Oisín in the Land of Youth is based, as regards the outlines of this remarkable story, on the LAOI OISÍN AR TIR NA N-ÓG, written by Michael Comyn about 1750, and edited with a translation by Thomas Flannery in 1896 (Gill & Son, Dublin). Comyn's poem was almost certainly based on earlier traditional sources, either oral or written or both, but these have not hitherto been discovered.

The History of King Cormac. The story of the birth of Cormac and his coming into his kingdom is to be found in SILVA GADELICA, where it is edited from THE BOOK OF BALLYMOTE, an MS. dating from about the year 1400.

The charming tale, of his marriage with Ethne ni Dunlaing is taken from Keating's FORUS FEASA. From this source also I have taken the tales of the Brehon Flahari, of Kiernit and the mill, and of Cormac's death and burial. The *Instructions of Cormac* have been edited and translated by Dr Kuno Meyer in the Todd Lecture Series of the Royal Irish Academy, xiv., April 1909. They are found in numerous MSS., and their date is fixed by Dr Meyer about the ninth century. With some other Irish matter of the same description they constitute, says Mr Alfred Nutt, "the oldest body of gnomic wisdom" extant in any European vernacular. (*FOLK-LORE*, Sept. 30, 1909.)

The story of Cormac's adventures in Fairyland has been published with a translation by Standish Hayes O'Grady in the *TRANSACTIONS OF THE OSSIANIC SOCIETY*, vol. iii., and is also given very fully by d'Arbois de Jubainvilie in his CYCLE MYTHOLOGIQUE IRLANDAIS. The tale is found, among other MSS., in the BOOK OF BALLYMOTE, but is known to have been extant at least as early as the tenth century, since in that year it figures in a list of Gaelic tales drawn up by the historian Tierna.

The ingenious story of the *Judgment concerning Cormac's Sword* is found in the BOOK OF BALLYMOTE, and is printed with a translation by Dr Whitly Stokes in *IRISCHE TEXTE*, iii. Serie, 7 Heft, 1891.

Pronouncing Index

The correct pronunciation of Gaelic proper names can only be learned from the living voice. It cannot be accurately represented by any combination of letters from the English alphabet. I have spared the reader as much trouble as possible on this score by simplifying, as far as I could, the forms of the names occurring in the text, and if the reader will note the following general rules, he will get quite as near to the pronunciation intended as there is any necessity for him to do. A few names which might present some unusual difficulty are given with their approximate English pronunciations in the Index.

The chief rule to observe is that vowels are pronounced as in the Continental languages, not according to the custom peculiar to England. Thus *a* is like *a* in *father*, never like *a* in *fate*, *I*(when long) is like *ee*, *u* like *oo*, or like *u* in *put* (never like *u* in *tune*). An accent implies length, thus *Dún*, a fortress or mansion, is pronounced *Doon*. The letters *ch* are never to be pronounced with a *t* sound, as in the word *chip*, but like a rough *h* or a softened *k*, rather as in German. *Gh* is silent as in English, and *g* is always hard, as in *give*. *C* is always as *k*, never as *s*.

In the following Index an accent placed after a syllable indicates that the stress is to be laid on that syllable. Only those words are given, the pronunciation of which is not easily ascertainable by attention to the foregoing rules.

INDEX

Æda	is to be pronounced	Ee'-da.
Ailill	"	Al'-yill.
Anluan	"	An'-looan.
Aoife	"	Ee'-fa.
Bacarach	"	Bac'-ara*h*.
Belachgowran	"	Bel'-a*h*-gow'-ran.
Cearnach	"	Kar'-na*h*.
Cuchulain	"	Coo-*h*oo'-lin.
Cumhal	"	Coo'wal, Cool.
Dacar	"	Dak'-ker.
Derryvaragh	"	Derry-var'-a.
Eisirt	"	Eye'sert.
Eochy	"	Yeo'*h*ee.
Fiachra	"	Fee'-a*k*ra
Fianna	"	Fee'-anna.
Finegas	"	Fin'-egas.
Fionnuala	"	Fee-on-oo'-ala, shortened in modern Irish into Fino'-la
Flahari	"	Fla'-haree.
Iorroway	"	Yor'-oway.
Iubdan	"	Youb'-dan.
Iuchar	"	You'-*h*ar.
Iucharba	"	You-*h*ar'-ba .
Liagan	"	Lee'-agan.
Lir	"	Leer
Logary	"	Lo'-garee

108

Maev	"	rhyming to *wave*.
Mananan	"	Man'-anan.
Mesgedra	"	Mes-ged'-ra.
Midir	"	Mid'-eer.
Mochaen	"	Mo-*h*ain'.
Mochaovóg	"	Mo-*h*wee'-vogue.
Moonremur	"	Moon'-ray-mur.
Oisín	"	Ush'-een (Ossian)
Peisear	"	Pye'-sar.
Sceolaun	"	Ske-o'-lawn (the *e* very short).
Slievenamuck	"	Sleeve-na-muck'
Slievenamon	"	Sleeve-na-mon'
Tuish	"	Too'-ish.

FOOTNOTES

[1]

CUCHULAIN, THE HOUND OF ULSTER. By Eleanor Hull.

[2]

There is one important tale of the Finn cycle, the *Pursuit of Dermot and Grania*, which I have not included. I have omitted it, partly because it presents the character of Finn in a light inconsistent with what is said of him elsewhere, and partly because it has in it a certain sinister and depressing element which renders it unsuitable for a collection intended largely for the young.

[3]

I gave this book—*The History of Ireland* (HEROIC PERIOD)—to Burne-Jones in order to interest him in Irish myth and legend. "I'll try and read it," he said. A week afterwards he came and said—It is a new world of thought and pleasure you have opened to me. I knew nothing of this, and life is quite enlarged. But now, I want to see all the originals. Where can I get them?"

I have only spoken of prose writing above. But in poetry (and in Poetry well fitted to the tales), this work had already been done nobly, and with a fine Celtic splendour of feeling and expression, by Sir Samuel Ferguson.

[4]

I speak here of the better known of the two versions of this encounter of the pagan with the Christian spirit. There are others in which the reconciliation is carried still further. One example is to be found in the *Colloquy of the Ancients* (SILVA GADELICA). Here Finn and his companions are explicitly pronounced to be saved by their natural virtues, and the relations of the Church and the Fenian warriors are most friendly.

[5]

Everything, on the contrary, in the Mythological Cycle is gifted with life, all the doings and things of nature are represented as the work of living creatures; but it is quite possible that those in Ireland who made these myths were not Celts at all.

[6]

I give one example of the way colour was laid on to animals just for the pleasure of it. "And the eagle and cranes were red with green heads, and their eggs were pure crimson and blue"; and deep in the wood the travellers found "strange birds with white bodies and purple heads and golden beaks," and afterwards three great birds, "one blue and his head crimson, and another crimson and his head green, and another speckled and his head gold."

[7]

This word is pronounced Shee, and means "the folk of the fairy mounds."

[8]

This is quoted with a few omissions, from Lady Gregory's delightful version, in her *Book of Saints and Wonders*, of an episode in *The Colloquy of the Ancients* (Silva Gadelica).

[9]

Pronounced Eefa.

[10]

Scotland. Inishglory is an island in the Bay of Erris, on the Mayo coast.

[11]

A magic banquet which had the effect of preserving for ever the youth of the People of Dana.

[12]

Pronounced Mo-chweev-ogue.

[13]

See p. 133, *note.*

[14]

Ballysodare = the Town of the Falls of Dara, in Co. Sligo.

[15]

Dundalk.

[16]

Blood-fine.

[17]

The Hill of Howth.

[18]

Cluan Tarbh, Clontarf; so called from the roaring of the waves on the strand.

[19]

The ancient royal residence of Ulster, near to the present town of Armagh.

[20]

I am much indebted to the beautiful prose translation of this song, published by Dr Kuno Meyer in *Ériu* (the Journal of the School of Irish Learning), Vol. I. Part II. In my poetic version an attempt has been made to render the riming and metrical effect of the original, which is believed to date from about the ninth century.

[21]

The hill still bears the name, Knockanar.

[22]

I have in the main borrowed Standish Hayes O'Grady's vivid and racy translation of these adages of the Fianna. (SILVA GADELICA, Engl. transl., p. 115.)

[23]

Ogham-craobh = "branching Ogham," so called because the letters resembled the branching of twigs from a stem. The Ogham alphabet was in use in Ireland in pre-Christian times, and many sepulchral inscriptions in it still remain.

[24]

Glanismole, near Dublin.

[25]

Talkenn or "Adze-head" was a name given to St Patrick by the Irish. Probably it referred to the shape of his tonsure.

[26]

Woad is a cruciferous plant, *Isatis tinctoria*, used for dyeing.

[27]

Pronounced Bweé-cad. His name is said to be preserved in the townland of Dunboyke, near Blessington, Co. Wicklow.

[28]

The Instructions of Cormac (Tecosa Cormaic) have been edited with a translation by Dr. Kuno Meyer in the Todd Lecture Series of the Royal Irish Academy, vol. xv., April 1909.

[29]

Scotland.

[30]

Pronounced Fla'-haree—accent on the first syllable.

[31]

The institution of fosterage, by which the children of kings and lords were given to trusted persons among their friends or followers to bring up and educate, was a marked feature of social life in ancient Ireland, and the bonds of affection and loyalty between such foster-parents and their children were held peculiarly sacred.

[32]

See Miss Hull's CUCHULAIN, THE HOUND OF ULSTER, p. 175. The pair were Mananan, god of the sea, and Fand his wife, of whom a tale of great interest is told in the Cuchulain Cycle of legends. The sea-cloak of Mananan is the subject of a magnificent piece of descriptive poetry in Ferguson's CONGAL.

[33]

The original from the BOOK OF BALLYMOTE (14th century) is given in O'Curry's MS. MATERIALS OF IRISH HISTORY, Appendix xxvi. I have in the main followed O'Curry's translation.

[34]

Angus Óg was really a deity or fairy king. He appears also in the story of Midir and Etain. *q.v.*

[35]

See the conclusion of the *Vengeance of Mesgedra*.

[36]

The image was doubtless of wood overlaid with gold.

[37]

There are still Wishing Stones, which are used in connexion with petitions for good or ill, on the ancient altars of Inishmurray and of Caher Island, and possibly other places on the west coast of Ireland.

[38]

This famous cemetery of the kings of pagan Ireland lies on the north bank of the Boyne and consists of a number of sepulchral mounds, sometimes of great extent, containing, in their interior, stone walled chambers decorated with symbolic and ornamental carvings. The chief of these mounds, now known as Newgrange, has been explored and described by Mr George Coffey in his valuable work NEWGRANGE, published by the Royal Irish Academy. *Brugh*=mansion.

[39]

These lines are taken from Sir S. Ferguson's noble poem, *The Burial of King Cormac*, from which I have also borrowed some of the details of the foregoing narrative.

Printed in Great Britain
by Amazon